Faith Under Fire

Faith Under Fire

DAVID C. COOPER

Cover Design: Mark Johnson
Cover Photography: Dan McClure

Library of Congress Catalog Card Number: 2001097313
ISBN: 0-87148-349-1
Copyright © 2001 by Pathway Press
Cleveland, Tennessee 37311
All Rights Reserved
Printed in the United States of America

Contents

Acknowledgments

I want to graciously acknowledge a number of special people who assisted me with this project.

First, I want to thank my wife, Barbie, for her inspiration to do the project and for her tireless efforts in reading and proofing the manuscript.

I also want to thank my office staff for their review of the manuscript and editorial contributions: Pam Copeland, Lisa Sanders, Hunter Carter and Barbara Ross. I deeply appreciate the editorial work provided by Kathleen McCook.

I want to thank my good friend Mark Johnson for his creative and inspiring artwork for the book cover.

Finally, I want to thank my spiritual family, the Mount Paran Church of God, for their loving support and for their partnership in ministry. Many of the teachings in this book were first delivered to my congregation, who welcomed them with great enthusiasm.

Introduction

Noted Christian apologist, G.K. Chesterton, once warned that when people stop believing anything, they are prepared to believe everything. Perhaps this time has come in America with an invasion of world religions, pseudo-Christian movements, cults, the occult and unchristian philosophies.

Pollster George Gallup Jr., said, "The problem is not that Americans don't believe, it's that they believe everything. Thus, we find in the extreme cases the weekly churchgoer who believes in channeling and the born-again Christian who believes in ghosts and witches. The question is how can churches help people discern what is of God and what is not?"

I have written this book as a historical and practical guide to help believers discern truth from error and understand other people's religious viewpoints. Such knowledge is vital for us to intelligently share our faith with people of other faiths. My purpose is not to criticize others in their spiritual pursuits, nor to demean other religions. Many well-meaning persons are misled spiritually in their genuine quest for God.

Humanity is incurably religious. Sigmund Freud even tried through psychoanalysis to cure us of what he called the "universal obsessive neurosis"—or our belief in God. He didn't succeed. Reinhold Niebuhr said, "Irreligion is a luxury which only those who observe life rather than live it may allow themselves. Those who live virtually must base their life upon an act of faith that life has meaning, and seek to conform their actions to that meaning."[1]

All religions share three common characteristics: beliefs, a code of conduct and worship. Religion boils down to our concept of God and how we experience Him. How we think about God, in turn, shapes our attitudes, values, beliefs, philosophy of life and, ultimately, our lifestyle.

There are three monotheistic religions in the world: Judaism, Christianity and Islam. (*Monotheism* means the belief in one God.) They all have their origins in the Old Testament patriarch, Abraham. He was the father of the Hebrew people. From Israel came Jesus the Messiah. His followers were later called Christians, although most early believers, like their Master, were Jewish. Christianity, then, is the natural outflow and fulfillment of Judaism. Finally, Mohammed blended elements of Judaism and the teachings of Christ along with his own religious roots to pioneer a new religion known as Islam.

The Eastern religions of Hinduism, and its later offshoot, Buddhism, are polytheistic religions. *Polytheism* means the belief in many gods, which includes everything from deities to inanimate objects to the elements of the universe. In Eastern mysticism, God may be seen as personal or impersonal, depending on the particular religious viewpoint. New Ageism, mysticism, astrology, transcendental meditation, and the belief in karma and reincarnation, all find their roots in the ancient eastern religions.

The American culture has also been impacted by two pseudo-Christian movements that began in the 1800s: Mormonism and Jehovah's Witnesses. Because they are unaware of the real beliefs espoused by these movements, many individuals believe they are Christian denominations. But a great divide exists on many fundamental points between orthodox Christian faith and these two particular movements.

America has its share of religious cults. There are about 700, according to one research study, with each one headed by a formidable leader claiming to be a prophet of God, or even worse, the Messiah himself. What is a cult? A cult is a religious movement that deviates from Biblical truth about the nature of God and His provision of salvation through Jesus Christ.

Cults share three basic characteristics. First, a cult is led by a charismatic leader claiming to be a representative of God. Second, cults claim secret revelations of truth known only to the adherents of the movement. Third, cults manipulate, exploit and control the thinking, lifestyle and financial resources of their members. Such groups often recruit followers by offering seminars on self-fulfillment rather than salvation on campuses and in corporate settings.

The most frequent sign Jesus gave of His second coming was the proliferation of false Christs and false prophets. "Many false prophets will appear and deceive many people. For false Christs and false prophets will appear and perform great signs and miracles to deceive even the elect—if that were possible" (Matthew 24:11, 24).

The issue is not whether all religions have some good points. Many do. There exists an obvious sharing of a collective morality among many religions. In addition, all the major religions welcome Jesus into their faith and ascribe to Him a status greater than that of an ordinary man. Even the Koran acknowledges His virgin birth, and considers Him to be one of the seven great prophets.

The issue is one of truth. What is the truth about God? About Jesus Christ? About life after death? About morality? And what is the source of truth? We will review world religions and the pseudo-Christian movements in light of the truth of the Bible.

Our goal is simple: To better understand the Christian faith along with other religious viewpoints, so that we can effectively share our faith when those special "divine opportunities" come our way.

Witnessing should not intimidate a believer. Think of it as simply sharing your personal testimony of what Christ means to you. You are the greatest living witness to the risen Christ! God not only wants you to be His witness, but to be an expert witness. Like a lawyer gets an expert witness to support his case in a court of law, so Jesus wants you to be an expert witness for Him. Expert witnesses are knowledgeable.

This book is not an exhaustive study of religions. Many other works have accomplished that task quite sufficiently. I have sought to provide a tool believers can use to better understand other religions so they can be expert witnesses for Christ.

When God gives you the opportunity to share your faith, be considerate and respectful of the viewpoints of others. Try to see life from their vantage point. Most people are raised in a particular religion. They have no reason to question its validity. Show the same respect and desire to listen as you have for wanting to share your faith.

Sharing one's faith requires a certain amount of courage. Religion is a sensitive subject and difficult to talk about. The Holy Spirit will give courage and the right words to say when the opportunity arises.

It is a privilege to share our faith. Cherish every opportunity that comes your way. I often think of Paul's encouragement when I have the opportunity to talk with someone about religious matters and to share Christ with them: "Be wise in the way you act toward outsiders; make the most of every opportunity. Let your conversation be always full of grace, seasoned with salt, so that you may know how to answer everyone" (Colossians 4:5, 6).

The Invasion of Islam

T he word *Islam* simply means "submission" or
"peace." Submission to the will of God is the
essence of the religion of Islam. It all began with
a young camel driver named *Ubu'l-Kassim*, who would
later be called Mohammed, which means, "one highly
praised." He pioneered the religion of Islam.

Mohammed was born in A.D. 570 in the city of
Mecca located in Arabia. Followers of Islam became
known as Muslims, which means "those who submit to
God." Although he was from the Koerish, the leading
tribe of Mecca, he knew the meaning of suffering. Both
his parents died before he was 6.

As a young man, he began working with caravans and
at 25, went to work for a wealthy widow named Khadija
as the manager of her caravan business. They eventually
married, although she was 15 years older than he was.
Some of her relatives were Christians. Her uncle, in fact,
was the bishop of the Nestorian church.

1

Mohammed spent considerable time in spiritual con-templation. He observed the lawlessness and wars among the Arabian tribes. He also questioned the validity of the Arabian animistic religion, which worshiped hundreds of false gods around a black stone called the *Kaaba.* Among these deities were angels, demons, and a chief god called *Al-eela* (the god).

Mohammed often prayed and meditated alone in a cave at Mount Hira, outside Mecca. He became engrossed with the name *Al-eela,* one of the Arabic deities who had no image. Later, the name was changed to *Allah,* which means God.

When he was 40 years old, he entered the cave at Hira where he claimed he was confronted by the angel Gabriel. While meditating on the name of Allah, he heard the angel's voice in the cave. Three times the voice command-ed him, "Proclaim!" After the third time Mohammed asked, "What shall I proclaim?" The answer is recorded in the Koran:

> Cry in the name of the Lord!
>   Who created man from a blood clot.
> Cry! Thy Lord is wondrous kind
>   Who by thy pen has taught mankind
> Things they knew not (being blind).

The experience terrified him, and he believed it to be demonic. Mohammed suffered periodic seizures that resulted in trance-like states. He questioned these as being either demonic or divine. His wife encouraged his metaphysical experiences and became his first convert.

During periodic visits to Hira Cave, Mohammed received additional revelations, and these constitute much of the Koran. He spent the next 22 years propagating his new religion and translating his oral teachings. They were later recorded in the Koran. Today, Islam is reported to be the fastest growing religion in the world.

The History of Islam

At first, few people accepted Mohammed's simple message. His teachings focused on sharing one's wealth with the poor to gain assurance of the afterlife and emphasized the Day of Judgment, which would bring severe punishment for the unbeliever. His denouncement of idol worship threatened the livelihood of businessmen in Mecca. As a result, followers of Mohammed were often beaten or stoned.

His own life was threatened in A.D. 622. He fled Mecca and went to Yathrib about 250 miles away. His flight is called the *Hegira*, and marks the beginning of the Muslim era. Yathrib was renamed *Medina*, meaning "the city of the prophet."

The followers of Mohammed assembled a fighting force and developed the concept of *jihad*, the holy war, which promises immediate entrance into paradise for those who die in battle. He ruled as a king and a prophet during this time after the *Hegira,* or flight, as he built his following.

In 628, Mohammed led his troops toward Mecca and conquered the city. Within 10 years after his *Hegira,* he controlled all of Arabia. In 632, four years after conquering

Mecca, he died in the arms of his favorite wife, Aisha, whom he married when she was only 7 years old.

A man named Abu Bakr succeeded Mohammed after his death, and established a system of religious leaders known as *caliphs.* This rise to power was marked by violent acts and murders as he exercised his newly-inherited powers.

Muslim armies, bent on conquest, spread Islam to India, North Africa and into Spain. The Battle of Tours (A.D. 732) prevented Islam from conquering all of Europe. With its capital in Baghdad, Islam established a regime that spread over three continents. The Islamic Empire lasted for 1,000 years.

Arabs developed the concept of algebra, designed the architectural pointed arch used in Europe's great cathedrals, and introduced to the West such produce as sugar, paper, apricots and rice. Constantinople (modern-day Istanbul, Turkey) became the capital of the Ottoman Empire, which lasted until the 20th century.[1]

The Prophets and the Koran

Islam reveres seven great prophets: Adam, Abraham, Moses, David, Solomon, Jesus and Mohammed. Mohammed is considered to be the last and greatest prophet possessing the full revelation of Allah. Only Jesus is referred to as sinless in the Koran, however. Even Mohammed had to repent of his sins.

The Koran mentions 25 prophets and Islam recognizes over 100,000 prophets, all supposedly carrying the same message. Other caliphs or successors have followed in Mohammed's steps.

The Koran is the sacred book of Islam. According to Muslim belief, God revealed Islam, the first religion, in three books: the Torah, the Psalms (*Zabur*) and the book of Jesus (*Injeel,* meaning, evangel). Man corrupted these books, they contend, so God sent the angel Gabriel to Mohammed with a new book, the Koran (*Qur'an*).

The Koran consists of three sections: Old Testament excerpts, New Testament excerpts, and Mohammed's revelations, which came to him over a period of 20 years. Mohammed himself did not actually write down his revelations. Muslims believe that God dictated every word of the Koran. For Muslims, the Koran is the only infallible word of God, which they believe has existed from eternity in a preserved tablet. The teachings of the Koran are supplemented by the traditions of the *Hadith*.

Islam considers the Bible to be a corrupted rule of faith inferior to Mohammed's message. The Koran contains a blend of various religious influences, however, including Arabian ceremonies and fasting regulations, Zoroastrian (Persian and Indian) beliefs, and strong elements of Judaism and Christianity.

Mohammed learned the religion of the Jews and Christians from at least two sources. First, Jews and Christians lived in his hometown of Mecca. Second, he encountered Jews and Christians during his travels with the caravan trade.

Practicing Islam

Muslims observe five spiritual disciplines in their practice of Islam as a way of life. First, the Islamic creed, called *Shahada,* states, "There is no God but Allah, and Mohammed is his prophet." Devout Muslims repeat the creed five times a day.

Second, prayer is offered five times a day (morning, noon, late afternoon, sunset and before bedtime). The prayer begins usually by reciting the first chapter of Koran, which takes about three minutes. Muslims gather for prayer in mosques at noon on every Friday, the holy day of the week. Sermons are delivered during the service.

Muslims wash their feet, arms and hands, as well as discard their shoes before entering the mosque. The posture for prayer is always kneeling, facing eastward toward Mecca. Originally, they faced toward Jerusalem, although Mohammed never actually visited Jerusalem. When the Jews rejected him as a prophet, he changed the direction to Mecca. A portion of the opening *surah* of the Koran reads:

King of the day of Judgment.
'Tis thee we worship and thee we ask for help.
Guide us in the straight path.
  The path of those whom thou hast favored,
Not the path of those who incur thine anger
  not of those who go astray.
He is not begotten nor does he beget.

Third, Ramadan celebrates Mohammed's initial commission and the revelation of the Koran. During this holy month, fasting lasts from sunrise to sunset. Eating and drinking occurs from the evening to the early morning hours. Ramadan also commemorates *Hegira,* Mohammed's famous flight from Mecca to Medina. Their fasting signifies self-discipline and submission to Allah.

Fourth, each Muslim is to make a pilgrimage to Mecca at least once during his lifetime to insure his salvation. While there he walks around the *Kabba,* a building that houses a sacred black stone, supposedly from Eden, which Gabriel is said to have brought to Earth. According to the myth, the *Kabba* was built originally by Abraham and Ishmael at the place where Abraham prayed first to God.

Finally, Muslims are required to give two-tenths of one percent of their income in Muslim countries to the poor. Also, freewill offering are given to the mosques.

Teachings and Practices

A number of important teachings and practices distinguish the life of a Muslim.

No God but Allah. Allah cannot be known, Muslims believe. They do not experience a personal relationship with God. He is transcendent (above and beyond creation) and not immanent (present with us). Islam discounts the doctrine of the Trinity as presented in both the Old and New Testaments. Allah has 99 known names represented on a rosary (worry beads); only the camel knows the 100th name.

Everything in life is predestined by Allah. One must be content with his lot in life and be grateful. Every event of life expresses Allah's will. When I was in Israel, my good friend Doron, who serves as a guide, told me about the Islamic view of the will of God. The Arabs often use the word *enchala,* which means, "If God wills." Everything is *enchala* to the Arab. Since everything is predetermined,

Arabs do not make commitments of time. An Arab can't commit to be somewhere tomorrow if it's not God's will, and he doesn't really know what is God's will.

The concept of God's will is distorted in Islam. Today, Saddam Hussein celebrates victory over the United States in the Kuwait invasion. Since George Bush Sr. is no longer president and Hussein is still in power, they believe they won the Gulf War. As far as they are concerned, the will of God was accomplished, in spite of the effects of the war on Iraq. The same is true for Syria. Despite losing the Six-Day War in 1967, they saw the results as the will of God. So, in their minds they won.

Concept of heaven. The only way for a Muslim to absolutely guarantee his entrance into Paradise is for him to be martyred. As Mohammed was dying, he claimed that Jews had poisoned him, and this gave him the status of a martyr. Soldiers are motivated to sacrifice themselves for Islam by the promise of everlasting life. One killed in battle is regarded as a martyr.

Heaven, for Muslims, means receiving everything they were denied in this life. Heaven is pictured with a river of liquor and Muslim men are surrounded by celestial maidens, called *houriyat,* and prepubescent girls, called *qasiraat.* Eternal judgment in hell awaits those whose evil deeds outweigh the good.

Missionary activity focuses on conquest rather than individual conversion. A nation is considered Muslim if those in political power are Muslim, regardless of whether or not the people are Muslim. Its missionary work aims to establish the kingdom of God over territories and countries by bringing the social, political and economic institutions under the rule of Allah. Missionary activity does not focus on personal conversion.

One deliberate strategy of proselytizing involves Muslim men marrying Christian women in non-Muslim countries. They then move the family back to the native country, making the household Muslim. Any children born into the household are automatically Muslim, according to Islamic law, and the father has sole rights over the children in a Muslim divorce.

People are divided into two categories—those who submit to Allah and those who resist his will. Those who resist can be the focus of missionary activity, financial hardship or even holy war, which is called *jihad*.

Ministry of angels. One of the ways Allah reveals His will is through angels. In Islam, the four archangels include *Gabriel*, who revealed the Koran; *Michael*, who supplies man's needs; *Asrafel*, who will blow his trumpet to announced the Day of Judgment; and *Asrael*, who examines men's souls at the Resurrection. Satan, who was expelled from Eden, is included among the angels because he refused to obey Adam and Allah.

The place of Jesus Christ. The Koran honors Jesus as a great prophet and testifies to His virgin birth. However, Muslims do not understand the Holy Spirit, even though the Koran records that the Spirit breathed upon Mary in the conception of Jesus. Islam discredits the crucifixion of Jesus. They cannot fathom God allowing His prophet to be treated so cruelly. Muslims believe Jesus was translated to heaven before the Crucifixion. Another man was mistaken for Jesus, they say, and was crucified in His place. But they believe that Jesus will return to earth in the last days to judge the world.

Role of women. Women possess only limited rights in orthodox Islam. A Muslim wife must live in total submission to the will of her husband. A man can divorce his wife by saying to her three times, "I divorce you." In a divorce, the husband exercises complete rights over all the children. While women are permitted to make the pilgrimage to Mecca, still they are not allowed to enter the *Kabba.*

Mohammed himself had 13 wives. The Koran teaches that it is customary for a man to have only four wives at a time, but he must treat each one with equal respect and care.

Women keep their heads covered and faces veiled. They wear the ankle-length *chador* in strict Muslim countries. In Turkey, however, the government is democratic, not Islamic. Women there are not permitted to observe the strict dress code. The purpose is to model a tolerance for religion, since Turkey is heavily influenced by Western culture. I point this out to underscore that diversity exists among Arab nations about how Islam influences national affairs.

The goal of Islam. The goal of Islam is to subject the entire world to Allah and his laws by force or persuasion. Not all Muslims support extreme and aggressive efforts, however. Some practice Islam in tolerance and brotherhood.

Jews and Christians. The Koran breathes both hot and cold toward Jews and Christians. Extreme Muslim fanatics decry the abomination of Jews and Christians, while moderate Muslims accept them as "the people of the Book."

The Koran states twice that, "Jews and Christians and whoever believes in God . . . and does what is right shall have nothing to fear or regret."

It is clear, however, that other Koran passages encourage Muslims to fight against Jews and Christians. Those who fight and die for Islam are promised everlasting life in paradise. The cost of conversion to Christianity for Muslims in strict countries is high. It can even mean death.

The supreme leader of Afghanistan's ruling Taliban militia warned on January 8, 2001, that his regime would enforce the death penalty on any Muslim who converts to another faith. Taliban leader Mullah Mohammed Omar made the declaration over Radio Shariat, explaining that such action is required by the strict interpretation of Islamic law enforced under Taliban rule. Taliban controls approximately 90 percent of Afghanistan at the time of this writing. Omar also said that "any non-Muslim found trying to win converts will also be killed," according to an Associated Press report on the broadcast.[2]

Such extremism bears fruit in terrorism waged in the name of Allah. On September 11, 2001, America became the object of extreme Muslim *jihad* when 19 terrorists highjacked four American airliners and crashed them into the World Trade Center and the Pentagon. One plane went down in Pennsylvania before reaching its target, which is believed to have been somewhere in Washington, D.C.

News sources revealed F.B.I. reports of a document found that provides insight into the twisted minds of these terrorists. Mohammed Atta, one of the key organizers of the attack, flew the first plane, American Flight 11 from Boston, into the World Trade Center. The FBI believes he also wrote the five-page handwritten document, in Arabic, to give final instructions to the other terrorists.

This document was later found in his luggage, which ironically was never placed on the plane in Boston. The document includes Islamic prayers, instructions for the last night of life and practical reminders to the hijackers to bring "knives, your will, IDs, your passport and finally, to make sure no one follows you." The following are excerpts from his instructions and prayers:

> Obey God, his messenger, and don't fight among your-selves, or you will be come weak; and stand fast, God will stand with those who stand fast . . . you should ask for guidance, you should ask God for help, pray through the night, continue to recite the Quran . . . the time of judgement has arrived. Hence we need to utilize those few hours to ask God for forgiveness. From there you will begin to live the happy life, the infinite paradise . . . keep a very open mind, an open heart of what you will face. You will be entering paradise, everlasting life.

He then offered this prayer to Allah:

> Oh God, open all doors for me, the God who answers prayer and answers those who seek you. I am asking for your help and forgiveness. . . . There is no God but Allah, I being a sinner. We are of God and to God we return.

This brutal act of terrorism costs nearly 6,000 innocent American lives and untold suffering in orphaned children, grief-stricken families and a national epidemic of anxiety.[3]

Today, people are sorting through their religious beliefs. I spoke to a man from Afghanistan recently who has been in America for 30 years. He wept as he shared with me his disgust over this tragedy. He reflected on how beautiful his land was many years ago before it was torn apart by war and religious fanatics. He is a medical doctor.

12

He told me, "I have always avoided the subjects of religion and politics with my patients, thinking that my only job was to provide medical care. But now I am speaking out for Christ to my patients, especially those who are Muslim. I have been a Christian for many years, but now I am passionate about my Christianity."

Sects of Islam

Three majors sects exist in Islam.[4] First, the *Wahhabi,* who began in the 18th century. This sect requires strict obedience to the Koran, as seen in Saudi Arabia's moralistic rule.

Second, the *Shiites* (a word meaning "partisans") claim to be the direct descendants of Mohammed and heirs to his spiritual leadership. While Mohammed had no sons who survived him, his cousin Ali, who married his daughter Fatima, is regarded by the Shiites as the prophetic successor. Shiites represent about a tenth of all Muslims. The late Ayatollah Khomeini of Iran was a member of this sect.

Third, the *Sunnis,* who claim to be from "the tradition of the Prophet," represent 90 percent of Muslims. They nominate their leaders in each community since Mohammed left no directives about prophetic succession. Islam, like most religions, represents a fragmented faith consisting of diverse sects, and this remains one of its strengths.

Two other offshoots need mentioning. First, *Sufism* is a small group of Muslims who emphasize the desire to know Allah personally through mystical union and experiences. The founder, Melvana Rumi, developed the school for the famous "whirling dervishes," a drug-induced dance art designed to bring dancers (exclusively young boys) into a mystical trance. I have toured Rumi's facilities located in Konya, Turkey.

Second, the *Black Muslim* movement began in 1913 by a North Carolina man named Timothy Drew. As an adult he moved to New Jersey and changed his name to Noble Drew Ali. This individual founded the Moorish-American Science Temples. After his death, Wallace Ford appeared on the scene claiming to be Ali's reincarnation.

Ford claimed to have been born in Mecca, and said he was sent to America to redeem the black man from the tyranny of the white man. One of his most prominent spokesmen, a charismatic leader, was Elijah Mohammed who helped him found the Nation of Islam. Later, Elijah Mohammed became the head of the organization.

A notable leader of the movement was Malcolm X who was the mouthpiece of Elijah Mohammed. He was murdered by one of Mohammed's rivals in 1965. The goal of the Black Muslim movement is to liberate African-Americans from social discrimination and to empower them for self-autonomy.

The original leaders also sought to establish a separate nation of African-Americans within the United States. They continue to oppose the integration and reconciliation message of the late Dr. Martin Luther King and other civil rights leaders. Their most outspoken leader today is Louis Farrakan.

Making an Impact on Muslims

Reaching Muslims for Christ begins with understanding how Muslims think about God and about salvation. They hold the following basic beliefs:

God cannot be known. He is transcendent. A verse like John 3:16, "For God so loved the world," contradicts everything a Muslim believes about God.

Religion is external, not internal. Islam focuses on ritual prayer offered five times a day, but not on an intimate communion with God. It reflects fearful submission to Allah versus loving obedience to God as Father, and follows religious and moral stipulations without true holiness of life.

Good works provide the pathway to salvation. The only way to fully guarantee entrance into paradise, however, is through martyrdom for the cause of Islam. The Muslim awaits in his grave the Day of Judgment when his works, not God's grace, will determine his final and eternal destiny.

While repentance is required, no understanding of God's forgiveness is provided. Islam offers no doctrine of salvation as the gift of God, thus salvation is always tenuous and uncertain.

To reach a Muslim for Christ, you must be aware of the tremendous price he must pay for converting. The Muslim who converts to Christianity in a strictly Muslim land stands to lose his identity, his family, his livelihood and possibly his life. Islam extremists view all other religions as satanic in origin.

Third, remember the different brands of Islam ranging from moderate to extreme. During Louis Farrakan's Million Man March on Washington, D.C. in 1995, several Muslim leaders denounced Farrakan's brand of Islam and refused to support the march. Christians need to be aware of the personal religious views of every Muslim with whom they share their faith.

Finally, use the secret weapon of the gospel—the love of God. A close friend of mine is a missionary in the Middle East. He has put his own life at risk by sharing Christ underground in strict Islamic states, such as Iraq. One day he went to a Syrian restaurant for lunch. After placing his order, the waiter said to him, "Can you tell me how to become a Christian?"

My friend was stunned by the question. He thought the waiter was just trying to build a relationship in order to obtain an American visa. So, he asked him,

"Aren't you a Muslim? Why do you want to become a Christian?"

The waiter responded, "I want to become a Christian because it is the religion of love."

2

Jesus and Judaism

The word *Judaism* comes from the Greek word *Ioudaismos* and refers to the religion and culture of the Jewish people. The word first appeared during the Intertestamental Period (c. 280 B.C. to 4 B.C.) by Greek-speaking Jews to distinguish their way of life and belief from that of the Greeks.

The patriarch Abraham was the father of the Hebrew nation. The word *Hebrew* is an English equivalent of the word *Habiru* meaning wanderer or sojourner, referring to the nomadic lifestyle of the Patriarchs. The later term *Jew* originally referred to those belonging to the tribe of Judah but later came to refer to anyone of the Hebrew race.

The history of the Jewish people is one marked by the fingerprints of God. They have endured rejection, invasion, captivity and dispersion; yet they occupy center stage in modern history.

God's covenant still stands: "I will make you into a great nation and I will bless you; I will make your name great, and you will be a blessing. I will bless those who bless you, and whoever curses you I will curse; and all peoples on earth will be blessed through you" (Genesis 12:2, 3).

During the reign of the Russian Czar Peter the Great, an elderly preacher was imprisoned for his faith. The Czar summoned him one day and asked, "Can you give me one infallible proof to verify the Bible?"

"Yes, Sire," he replied, "the Jew."

Former President Harry Truman said that the most important action he performed while in office was to sign the agreement recognizing Israel as an independent state.

A Holy History

Jewish history is, in reality, a story of faith. Their history can be traced along the following timeline:

2,000 B.C.	Abraham is called in the Ur of Chaldees to go to the Promised Land.
1,450 B.C.	The Exodus occurs under the leadership of Moses.
1,400 B.C.	Joshua leads in the conquest of Canaan.
1,380 B.C.	The Judges rule Israel for a period of 330 years.
1,053 B.C.	Saul is inaugurated as the first Israeli king.
1,013 B.C.	The Davidic kingdom is established and the covenant is given.
930 B.C.	Israel is divided after Solomon's death.
722 B.C.	Israel (the Northern kingdom) is invaded by Assyria and dispersed.
586 B.C.	Judah (the Southern kingdom) is invaded by Babylon and exiled.

539 B.C.	The Jews returned to Jerusalem after 70 years of Babylonian captivity.
165 B.C.	The Jews rededicate the Temple after defeating the Syrians (Hanukkah).
63 B.C.	Rome rises to power and annexes Israel.
A.D. 70	Rome destroys Jerusalem and the Temple under General Titus; the battle at Massada takes place.
A.D. 135	Hadrian the Roman invades Israel and renames it Palestine.
A.D. 1882	The first group of Jewish colonists settle in Palestine.
A.D. 1914	England, France, and Russia declare war on Ottoman Turks.
A.D. 1917	British forces under General Allenby advance into Palestine.
A.D. 1918	The Balfour Declaration is signed. The British guarantee a Jewish state.
A.D. 1948	The United Nations recognizes Israel as an independent state.
A.D. 1948	A War of Independence is fought against five Arab states.
A.D. 1956	The Sinai Campaign is fought against Egypt, Jordan and Syria.
A.D. 1967	The Six-Day War results in the Jews recapturing the city of Jerusalem.
A.D. 1973	The Yom Kippur (Day of Atonement) War is fought.
A.D. 2000	Great civil unrest and violence break out between Jews and Palestinians. The peace accord is threatened.

The Jewish religion has developed through a series of historical stages including the Patriarchal Period (Genesis), the Mosaic Period and the Law, the Intertestamental Period (c. 400 B.C. to 4 B.C.), the Rabbinical Period (during the time of Jesus), the Medieval Period, and, finally the Modern Period.

The result is a unified Jewish faith consisting of diverse groups. *Orthodox Jews* maintain strict adherence to the law and rabbinical tradition. *Reformed Jews* represent a strong reaction to orthodoxy. *Conservative Jews* represent a blend of orthodox and reformed teachings. *Secular Jews* do not actively practice the faith of Judaism. *Messianic Jews* accept Jesus as the Messiah and Lord.

Fundamentals of Faith

Jewish religious beliefs are rooted in two main bodies of literature: the Old Testament, especially the Mosaic Law (the *Torah*), and the Talmud. The Talmud consists of oral tradition and law developed during the Intertestamental Period and reflects the teachings of the rabbis. The Talmud includes the *Mishnah*, a written record of oral law dated around A.D. 200 and edited by Rabbi Judah ha-Nasi; and the *Gemara*, a rabbinical commentary on the *Mishnah* completed in A.D. 500. The Talmud contains over 6,000 folio pages and is the work of over 2,000 scholars.

Judaism is large enough to encompass a diversity of religious beliefs and traditions. This is seen in the marked differences between the Pharisees, Sadducees and Essenes during the time of Christ.

Traditionally, more emphasis has been placed on *deed* (*miswa*) than the *creed* (*ani ma'amin,* meaning, "I believe").

The Mishna (Abot 1:2) presents a broad philosophy characteristic of the early rabbis: "By three things is the world sustained: by the law, by the [temple] service and by deeds of lovingkindness." The essence of Judaism is found in God's requirement to "act justly and to love mercy and to walk humbly with your God" (Micah 6:8).

Faith is nurtured in the synagogue, which exists as a house of *study* (to learn the Torah), a house of *prayer* (to worship God), and a house of *assembly* (to cultivate community life). Interestingly, the role of the synagogue is the same as the role of the church, which exists to proclaim the *Word of God,* to *worship* God and to seek the *welfare* of the community in the church and the world.

There are four foundational pillars of Judaism. First, the Torah or the law of God is viewed as a living law. The written Torah is understood in light of the oral Torah. Second, there is one God, who is spiritual and eternal. Third, the people of Israel exist as one family with a corporate personality. Finally, the land God promised to Abraham is guaranteed for all generations.

Since Judaism focuses heavily on the way a Jew is to live, what are the basic principles of life?

First, man is pivotal in the universe as a partner with God in the unending process of creation. The rabbis teach, "God needs man as much as man needs God."

Second, man is a responsible moral agent, free to make his own choices, yet he is ultimately accountable to God.

Third, human progress is achieved by realizing the human potential. The nature of man is essentially good, capable of rising above the tendencies of sin. Humanity can be hopeful and optimistic about the future.

Fourth, Judaism focuses more on life "here-and-now" versus "then-and-there" in eternity. Earth and man constitute a greater concern than God and heaven. Thoughts about life after death have never occupied a major position in Jewish thought.

Fifth, all of life is sacred. Man is to seek the imitation of God in sanctifying every area of his life.

Sixth, man is to seek peace, justice and righteousness—themes that occupy a central place in the Old Testament. We are responsible for improving society through good deeds. While traditional Judaism views the Messiah as God's anointed human representative who will usher in a golden age, reformed Judaism teaches that the Messianic Age will transpire when humankind reaches a level of enlightenment, peace and justice.[1]

The Most Influential Jew Who Ever Lived

Where does Jesus fit into Judaism? First, Jesus was born of Jewish descent through the lineage of King David (Matthew 1:1-16; Luke 3:23-38). Paul underscores Jesus' Jewish ancestry when he describes the privileges of Israel (Romans 9:4, 5).

There is really no way to talk about the history of Judaism, without talking about Jesus. After all, Jesus is the most influential Jew who has ever lived. He has made the greatest impact on the world of any religious or political leader. Over one-third of the world's six billion people worship Jesus as Messiah and Lord. Christianity is the world's largest religion all because of the incredible influence of a Jewish rabbi named Jesus of Nazareth. Christianity itself began as a sect of Judaism (see Acts 9:2).

Jesus was recognized as a rabbi and given the honor and privileges of that standing. He preached and taught in the synagogues. Other rabbinical leaders confirmed His rabbinical authority and accepted the validity of His miracles (see John 3:1, 2). Some were His secret disciples.[2]

People came in droves to hear Jesus teach. "No one ever spoke the way this man does," the Temple guards said of Him (John 7:46). "The people were amazed at his teaching, because he taught them as one who had authority, not as the teachers of the law" (Mark 1:22).

Jesus' authority distinguished Him from other rabbis. Even the chief priests and elders recognized His authority. "'By what authority are you doing these things?' they asked. 'And who gave you this authority?'" (Matthew 21:23).

What was the basis of Christ's authority? First, He spoke as the Son of God. He referred to Himself often as the Son of Man, a messianic title used 86 times in the Gospels. Jesus openly revealed His divinity and received the worship of the people (Matthew 2:2; 21:1-11; 28:9, 17). He declared, "Before Abraham was born, I am!" It nearly got Him stoned because He was claiming to be one with God (John 8:58, 59). The words "I Am," come from the burning bush experience of Moses (Exodus 3:14). Moses identified the God of Israel by His covenant name *Yahweh,* meaning "the Promise Keeper."

Jesus and The Law. His authority also came from His elevation of the Scripture over the traditions of the rabbis. He confronted the error of those who sought to place rabbinical tradition on the same level as Scripture.

23

And why do you break the command of God for the sake of your tradition? . . . Thus you nullify the word of God for the sake of your tradition. You hypocrites! Isaiah was right when he prophesied about you: "These people honor me with their lips, but their hearts are far from me. They worship me in vain; their teachings are but rules taught by men" (Matthew 15:3, 6-9).

Jesus stressed the authority of the Old Testament and refuted any rabbinical teaching that held the people in bondage to legalism. "You are in error," He told the Sadducees, "because you do not know the Scriptures or the power of God" (Matthew 22:29).

Jesus never took issue with the Old Testament. He upheld its authority as the Word of God. He clarified the Scripture because its meaning had been buried under a pile of rabbinical tradition. The people were unable to distinguish between God's word and the traditions of the rabbis. Jesus said, "Do not think that I have come to abolish the Law or the Prophets; I have not come to abolish them but to fulfill them" (Matthew 5:17).

Jesus summed up the Law and Prophets in two great commands: "Love the Lord your God with all your heart . . . soul . . . and with all your mind," and "Love your neighbor as yourself" (see Matthew 22:37-40; also Deuteronomy 6:5, Leviticus 19:18). The true goal of Judaism, then, is to live in right relationship with God and man. In this same way, the gospel of Christ reconciles man to God and man to man through Jesus Christ.

Jesus and Salvation. The doctrine of salvation is the same in both the Old and New Testaments. This is a common point of misunderstanding. Some assume (incorrectly, I might add) that people were saved in the Old Testament by keeping the Law and saved by grace through faith in the New Testament. Nothing could be further from the truth.

Salvation has never come through keeping the Law—either the law of God or the tradition of the rabbis. The Pharisees, during the Intertestamental Period, were the first to teach that entrance into the kingdom of God required one to know the law and keep the law. In contrast, the Old Testament teaches that salvation comes through faith in the grace of God, not by good works or religious rituals.

In John 3:1-15, Jesus told a Pharisee named Nicodemus, "I tell you the truth, no one can see the kingdom of God unless he is born again."

"How can a man be born when he is old?" Nicodemus asked.

Jesus answered, "Just as Moses lifted up the snake in the desert, so the Son of Man must be lifted up, that everyone who believes in him may have eternal life" (vv. 4, 5, 15).

Jesus is referring to the Old Testament account of Moses who used a bronze serpent in the wilderness as an illustration of God's judgment against sin through a substitutional offering. This same kind of imagery appears throughout the Old Testament. God provided garments of animal skins to cover Adam and Eve. God provided a ram on Mount Moriah in Isaac's place. God provided the Passover Lamb in Egypt. God taught the Israelites to offer a sacrifice every year on the Day of Atonement.

All these sacrifices pointed to Jesus, the true Lamb of God who takes away the sins of the world. God provides salvation by grace. We receive it by faith. Judaism did not begin as a religion of law, it began as a religion of faith. Abraham, "believed the Lord, and [God] credited it to him as righteousness" (Genesis 15:6).

The Law was given to provide the new nation established under Moses' leadership a system of government, civil law, morality and worship. The purpose of the Law, however, was never to make men right with God.

Paul says, "The law was put in charge to lead us to Christ that we might be justified by faith" (Galatians 3:24). The Old Testament prophet Habakkuk declared, "the righteous will live by his faith" (2:4). That statement appears throughout the New Testament to show the way of salvation (see Romans 1:17; Galatians 3:11; Hebrews 10:38, 39). The only way to become righteous, meaning "right with God," is by faith in the grace given us in Jesus Christ.

Jesus and the Sacrifices. Not only did the Law not make men righteous, neither did the sacrificial system of the Temple worship. Old Testament sacrifices, in and of themselves, did not atone for sins. Forgiveness comes through our confession and repentance of sins (1 John 1:9).

The Old Testament sacrifices served two purposes in the worship of Israel. First, they demonstrated God's provision of grace. The sacrifices, then, pointed forward to the day when the Messiah would make the ultimate sacrifice for the sins of the world. Second, the sacrifices represented the worshiper himself. He was vicariously dedicating himself to God as represented in the sacrifice.

26

Atonement is solely the work of God as seen in the exodus of Israel from Egypt. God redeemed His people from Egypt by His power and the blood of the Passover Lamb. Redemption, then, came by power and blood. The very act of putting the blood of the Passover lamb on the doorpost of every house was an act of faith on Israel's part in what God would do on their behalf.

The prophets condemned the practice of offering sacrifices apart from personal confession of sin and faith in God. Samuel said, "To obey is better than sacrifice" (1 Samuel 15:22). When David repented of his affair with Bathsheba, he prayed, "You do not delight in sacrifice, or I would bring it; you do not take pleasure in burnt offerings. The sacrifices of God are a broken spirit; a broken and contrite heart, O God, you will not despise" (Psalm 51:16, 17).

God asked Israel, "Do I eat the flesh of bulls or drink the blood of goats? Sacrifice thank offerings to God, fulfill your vows to the Most High, and call upon me in the day of trouble; I will deliver you, and you will honor me" (50:13-15). God spoke through Isaiah to the people, "Stop bringing meaningless offerings!" (Isaiah 1:13). Jeremiah rebuked the people in his day for trusting in the Temple service yet living in unbelief and disobedience (Jeremiah 7:1-15).

What good is a sacrifice if you don't love your neighbor? Or repent of your sins? Or care for the poor and oppressed? Or seek to obey God with all your heart?

Jesus fulfilled the sacrificial system of the Old Testament. It is no longer needed. Who needs the symbol when you have the reality? Jesus often spoke of the necessity of His death as the fulfillment of the sacrificial system. "For even the Son of Man did not come to be served, but to serve, and to give his life as a ransom for many" (Mark 10:45).

Isaiah foresaw the Messiah's sufferings:

> He was pierced for our transgressions, he was crushed for our iniquities; the punishment that brought us peace was upon him, and by his wounds we are healed. We all, like sheep, have gone astray, each of us has turned to his own way; and the Lord has laid on him the iniquity of us all (Isaiah 53:5, 6).

Who is this sin-bearer, of whom Isaiah speaks? Who is this Passover lamb who bore the iniquity of Jew and Gentile alike? Rabbinical tradition teaches that this prophecy speaks of the persecution and oppression suffered by the Israeli nation, with specific reference to the Babylonian exile. Jesus, however, announced its fulfillment in His crucifixion.

After His resurrection He told the disciples:

> Everything must be fulfilled that is written about me in the Law of Moses, the Prophets and the Psalms. This is what is written: The Christ will suffer and rise from the dead on the third day, and repentance and forgiveness of sins will be preached in his name to all nations, beginning at Jerusalem (Luke 24:44, 46, 47).

Jesus and the Covenants. The *covenant* concept is central in Scripture. God is a covenant-making and keeping God. Israel is the covenant people of God. Eight covenants are provided in Scripture: the covenant of Eden (Genesis 1:28-30); Adam's covenant (3:14-19); Noah's covenant (8:20-9:17); Abraham's covenant (12:1-3); Moses and the covenant of the law (Exodus 19:1-8); the Palestinian covenant promising the land of Canaan (Deuteronomy 30:1-4); David's covenant (2 Samuel 7:4-17); and the New Covenant (Jeremiah 31:31-34).

Four of these covenants are eternal: the Abrahamic covenant, the Palestinian covenant, the Davidic covenant and the New Covenant. They are based on God's grace and secured by His own eternal decree. They can never be altered. The covenants are literal, unconditional and provisional for Israel and the nations of the world. The covenants declare what God has willed to do on our behalf.

Look at the four eternal covenants closer. The Abrahamic covenant promises Israel a *seed* and a *land*. The Palestinian covenant expounds on the land promises of the Abrahamic covenant. The Davidic covenant promises an eternal *house,* a *kingdom* and a *throne* for David's descendants. The Old Testament prophets believed the promise of an eternal throne to David was a reference to the Messiah's throne.[3] Isaiah's prophecy of the Messiah's kingdom is, without question, the fulfillment of the Davidic covenant:

> For to us a child is born, to us a son is given, and the government will be on his shoulders. And he will be called Wonderful Counselor, Mighty God, Everlasting Father, Prince of Peace. Of the increase of his government and peace there will be no end. He will reign on David's throne and over his kingdom, establishing it and uphold-

ing it with justice and righteousness from that time on and forever. The zeal of the Lord Almighty will accomplish this (Isaiah 9:6, 7).

Finally, the New Covenant promised by Jeremiah, provides forgiveness for sins through the grace of God. Jesus connected the meaning of the Passover meal and the New Covenant in what we now call the Lord's Supper.[4] Jesus is the fulfillment of all the Old Testament covenants. They all pointed to the final one—the New Covenant.

Why did the Old Covenant need to be superseded by the New Covenant of Christ? The Old Testament sacrifices reminded worshipers of their sins. Only Christ's sacrifice can cleanse the conscience of the worshiper, enabling him to come to God in confidence.[5] The Old Covenant was *external,* based on ritualism; *powerless,* reflecting the people's inability to keep the law; and *temporary,* pointing forward to God's plan for the old to give way to the new. The New Covenant is the final covenant; it reconciles man to God: *amen*

> But God found fault with the people and said: "The time is coming, declares the Lord, when I will make a new covenant...." By calling this covenant "new," he has made the first one obsolete; and what is obsolete and aging will soon disappear. For this reason Christ is the mediator of a new covenant, that those who are called may receive the promised eternal inheritance (Hebrews 8:8, 13; 9:15).

Jesus and Prophecy. Jesus has fulfilled every Old Testament messianic prophecy, type and symbol pointing to Him. He has fulfilled all of the Law, the sacrifices, the

30

Temple service, the covenants, and the prophecies of the Messiah. Jesus fulfilled 300 Old Testament prophecies in His first coming. Let's consider a few:

Genesis 12:3—He would be born the seed of Abraham.

2 Samuel 7:12—He would be born the seed of King David.

Micah 5:2—He would be born in Bethlehem.

Isaiah 7:14—He would be born of a virgin.

Isaiah 9:1, 2—He would be a light for the Gentiles.

Isaiah 11:1—He would be called a Nazarene.

Isaiah 53:5—He would suffer a cruel death.

Isaiah 53:9—He would be buried with the rich.

Zechariah 9:9—He would enter Jerusalem on a donkey.

Zechariah 11:12—He would be betrayed for 30 pieces of silver.

Psalm 22:18—His enemies would gamble for His garments at His crucifixion.

Psalm 34:20—Not a bone of His body would be broken at the Cross.

Psalm 22:1—He would pray, "My God, why have you forsaken me?"

Psalm 16:10—He would rise from the dead.

Psalm 24:7-10—He would ascend into heaven.

Truly, "The testimony of Jesus is the spirit of prophecy" (Revelation 19:10).

Israel and the Church

What was true of the call of Israel is true of the church. Israel is called "a kingdom of priests" (Exodus 19:6). Peter uses this verse to identify the church as a "royal priesthood, a holy nation" (1 Peter 2:9). The prophet Hosea foretold the grafting of the Gentiles into the covenant (Hosea 1:10; 2:23).

Paul goes so far as to call the church "the Israel of God" (Galatians 6:16). This does not mean that God has abandoned His plan for the nation of Israel; He has not. However, the covenant of Abraham promised a blessing for "all peoples on earth" (Genesis 12:3).

There is no mistaking the connection between Israel and the church in the New Testament. Gentile believers are branches grafted into Israel the vine (Romans 11:17). Christ has destroyed the dividing wall between Jews and Gentiles, making one new man out of the two (Ephesians 2:11-22). Christians are also children of Abraham and heirs of the promise God gave him (Galatians 3:6, 7, 11, 26).

One of the most radical statements Paul makes concerns what it means to really be a Jew. He says that the true Jew is one who is circumcised in his heart not just in the flesh, "for not all who are descended from Israel are Israel" (Romans 9:6; see 2:28, 29). Judaism is a matter of the heart, not just one's natural lineage.

James the apostle addressed the church as "the twelve tribes scattered among the nations" (James 1:1). At the time he wrote the letter, there were no 12 tribes. He uses an analogy between the dispersion of the Jews and the church, which had been scattered because of persecution.

The people of God, Jew and Gentile alike, are portrayed in the Book of Revelation through a series of symbols using multiples of 12, a number which represents the people of God, based on the 12 tribes of Israel and the 12 apostles of Christ. The symbols include the 24 elders (Revelation 4:10), the 144,000 who are sealed by God (7:4-8; 14:1-5), and the New Jerusalem bearing the names of the 12 tribes of Israel and the 12 apostles (21:1-5, 12-14).

Originally, first-century Jewish Christians worshiped in the synagogues. Christianity was as a sect of Judaism called "the Way" (Acts 9:2). Christianity and Judaism parted company due to the persecution of Christians, launched initially by the Sanhedrin and Saul of Tarsus. Later, Christianity became more heavily identified with Gentiles, as more and more Gentiles became followers of Jesus.

Interestingly, the commission of the church corresponds to God's call to Israel. God chose Israel to witness of the one true God in a pagan world (Deuteronomy 6:4-9); to demonstrate the blessings of serving and obeying Him (Psalm 144:15); to preserve the Word of God from generation to generation (145:1-7); to prepare for the coming of the Messiah (Isaiah 40:1-3); to be a kingdom of priests (Exodus 19:6); and to live a lifestyle of love for God and neighbor for all nations to emulate (Genesis 12:1-3).

The gospel of Christ is the power of God unto salvation for everyone who believes, but "first for the Jew" (Romans 1:16). Christ told His disciples to begin their worldwide witness "at Jerusalem" (Luke 24:47). The church has a responsibility to carry the gospel of Jesus to Israel.

Is Jesus Israel's Messiah?

The fundamental difference between Christianity and Judaism concerns the person and ministry of Jesus, the Messiah. Judaism, except for Messianic Jews, does not accept Jesus as God's promised Messiah. They still await Messiah's coming.

The belief in the Messiah provides the spiritual thread that runs from Genesis to Revelation. It is obvious, however, when reading the Gospels that Jesus' concept of his messianic mission was not harmonious with the popular Jewish expectations of His day.

The word *Messiah* is a Greek translation of the Aramaic *mesiha*, derived from the Hebrew word *mashah*, meaning "to anoint, or to smear with oil." The title *Messiah* means the "anointed one." The English word *Christ* comes from the Greek *Christos,* meaning *Messiah.*

The Messianic Expectation

What did Israel expect her messiah to be and to do? Israel's hope for a king and a kingdom was reignited when the remnant from Babylon returned to their homeland under the leadership of Zerubbabel in 539 B.C. This leader was a descendant of David, who was appointed governor of the new state of Israel after the Babylonian exile.

Although the city of Jerusalem was restored and the Temple was rebuilt, it soon became apparent that Zerubbabel was not another David. So, the hope for Messiah was projected into the future. Eventually, it would be projected in the far and distant future—to the end of the age.

This became the prevailing mood as seen in the later Old Testament writings. Jeremiah foretold a continuation of the Davidic line (Jeremiah 33). Isaiah prophesied the glory of the coming Davidic king (Isaiah 9, 11). Micah announced the birth of the Davidic king in Bethlehem (Micah 5:2). Zechariah described the majesty of Messiah's kingdom in the last days (Zechariah 9; 12).

These prophecies were more than mere human hope; they represented the voice of God, which spoke to the Virgin Mary: "Give him the name Jesus. He will be great and will be called the Son of the Most High. The Lord God will give him the throne of his father David, and he will reign over the house of Jacob forever; his kingdom will never end" (Luke 1:31-33).

Before Jesus came, several different interpretations concerning the Messiah developed. Many rabbis believed there would be two Messiahs: Davidic Messiah, who would rule as king, and a Levitical Messiah, who would serve as priest. But by the time Jesus came, the prominent view was only in a Davidic Messiah.

How did they envision the Messiah? We get a description of him in Psalm 17 of the Apocryphal book, *Psalms of Solomon.* First, they expected him to be an earthly king over the nation of Israel championing her cause in world affairs. Second, the title "Messiah" was first used in a proper sense, meaning that the title and the messianic concept had been merged together. Third, the Messiah would be upright in all His ways and His hope would be in the Lord. Fourth, the capital of His kingdom would be Jerusalem, which would endure forever.

This is what the people expected the Messiah to be and to do when he appeared. During the time of Christ, the Messianic kingdom had become a composite picture derived from Old Testament and apocryphal sources. Here's a list of what the people had come to expect:

- Elijah would return to be the forerunner of the Messiah.

- The messianic age would begin with the travail of the Messiah.

- The new age would be a time of terror at the Day of the Lord, a time of cosmic upheaval and a time of complete disintegration of the universe itself and all relationships.

- It would be a time of divine judgment.

- Gentile nations would either be judged or redeemed, depending on different theological perspectives.

- There would be an ingathering of Israel back to her homeland from all nations.

- Jerusalem would be restored and given a new Temple.

- The dead would be raised.

- The new age of the Kingdom would endure forever.

- A complete restoration of all things would occur including a reuniting of the divided kingdom, abundant agricultural fertility, the end of all war and strife, peace between man and the animal kingdom, the removal of all sickness, pain, sorrow and death, and a climax of holiness and righteousness.[6]

By the dawn of the Christian era, the majority of Jews shared the belief in the coming of a mighty Messiah-warrior from David's lineage. The Qumran Covenanters and the Zealots shared this view and were eagerly anticipating his appearance to free them from the yoke of Roman oppression.

This explains why Jesus did not refer to Himself as Messiah and encouraged others to refrain from doing so. Although He certainly knew He was the Messiah, it was not until His trial before Caiaphas, the high priest, that He openly declared Himself to be Messiah (Mark 14:61, 62).

The reason for this is clear: the people expected the Messiah to usher in a political-military kingdom by force. But Jesus knew His messianic mission was to establish the kingdom of God in the hearts of all people. The kingdom of God would only come through His crucifixion, resurrection and ascension.

At Caesarea Philippi, Peter made the confession, "You are the Christ, the Son of the living God" (Matthew 16:16). Jesus then "warned his disciples not to tell anyone that he was the Christ. From that time on Jesus began to explain to his disciples that he must go to Jerusalem and suffer many things . . . he must be killed and on the third day be raised to life" (vv. 20, 21).

Jesus' Kingdom Message

Jesus saw the work of salvation and Messiah's mission as being one and the same. "For even the Son of Man did not come to be served, but to serve, and to give his life as a ransom for many" (Mark 10:45). The Jewish perspective of the Messiah was limited. They could only envision a political kingdom. But Jesus emphasized that the deliverance that the Messiah would bring would first be deliverance from the oppression of sin.

In this kind of environment, the Jewish people longed for a Messiah to deliver them from Roman oppression and to establish the Davidic kingdom of old. And into this kind of environment Jesus came. While He deliberately avoided using the title "Messiah," He did speak openly of Himself as the Son of Man, and boldly announced that by His very presence in the world, "The kingdom of God is near" (Mark 1:15).

When Jesus announced that the kingdom was already here, you can understand why it caught the attention of everyone who heard Him. The news of His kingdom message rang out as a message of hope. There existed a high level of messianic expectation among the people who envisioned a kingdom of vast economic, political and military power that would overthrow Rome and usher in the glory of the Davidic kingdom.

Such expectation was in order. For centuries Israel suffered under Gentile world powers—even as the prophet Daniel foresaw in his apocalyptic visions. Now, with Jesus on the scene, all of this was about to change, they thought.

Rome had installed Herod as king over Israel. Herod the Great was partly Jewish and partly Idumean. But he served the interests of Rome, not the Jews. During the days of Jesus, Israel was considered a Roman territory. The Antonio Fortress, where Pilate ruled as governor, was constructed next to the Temple.

Roman authority controlled Herod along with the Temple party of the Sadducees, the party of the priests. Israel was heavily taxed. Many of the people lived in abject poverty. It was a time of darkness—economically, socially, politically and spiritually. The people longed for the Messiah to come and to deliver them.

It was to a desperate people that Jesus announced, "The kingdom of God is near!" No wonder they came in droves to hear Him preach the good news of the kingdom. The most radical statement he made concerning the kingdom was, "The kingdom of God is within you" (Luke 17:21).

His kingdom would not come with military might, political power or religious aristocracy. His kingdom would not be measured by lands conquered, by subjects and slaves, or by wealth and power. His kingdom would not be centered in the Holy City Jerusalem. It would not be centered on the Seven Hills of Rome or in Babylon. His kingdom belonged to everyone who believed in Him: "To all who received him, to those who believed in his name, he gave the right to become children of God" (John 1:12).

Not only did He announce the arrival of the kingdom, He demonstrated its power by driving out demons, healing the sick, and performing miracles (see Matthew 4:17-25). He said, "But if I drive out demons by the Spirit of God, then the kingdom of God has come upon you" (12:28).

The Messianic Secret

While Jesus spoke openly about the kingdom, he also described its mystery element. He privately told His disciples, "The secret of the kingdom of God has been given to you" (Mark 4:11).

This "messianic secret" was simply the mystery by which the kingdom of God would come—not through military force or a political insurrection but through Christ's death, resurrection and ascension. The Holy Spirit would be sent to empower His disciples as representatives of the Kingdom. The kingdom of God came with power when Jesus rose from the dead (see Mark 9:1; Romans 1:4).

After the Holy Spirit came to believers on the Day of Pentecost, the secret of the Kingdom, that is, the good news of salvation, would be openly proclaimed to all nations (Matthew 24:14; Acts 1:8). The Cross was the "secret of the kingdom." The Cross was the predetermined will of God, agreed on before the Creation of the world (see 1 Peter 1:18- 20).

As Messiah, Jesus is both Daniel's "son of man" (see Daniel 7:13, 14) and Isaiah's "suffering servant" (Isaiah 53:1- 12). The early church preached that the kingdom of God is entered into through faith in Jesus (Acts 2:36; 28:31; John 3:3).

Not only is the Kingdom a present reality, but it is also a future promise. Today, we experience the earnest of the Kingdom. When Christ returns, we will experience the full blessings of the Kingdom. "The kingdom of the world has become the kingdom of our Lord and of his Christ, and he will reign for ever and ever" (Revelation 11:15). When Christ returns, every prophecy about the messianic kingdom will be fulfilled.

Israel in Bible Prophecy

The rebirth of Israel in 1948 is one of the most significant and important prophecies to be fulfilled in our time. What will be the final destiny of Israel? The apostle Paul foresaw the day of Israel's salvation as he echoed the words of the prophet Isaiah: "The deliverer will come from Zion; he will turn godlessness away from Jacob. And this is my covenant with them when I take away their sins" (Romans 11:26, 27).

He goes on to say concerning Israel: "God's gifts and his call are irrevocable" (v. 29). God's purpose for Israel continues today as He prepares her and the world for Messiah's return. Isaiah gave a preview of Christ's return and Israel's place in the messianic kingdom:

> Many people will come and say, "Come let us go up to the mountain of the Lord, to the house of the God of Jacob. He will teach us his ways, so that we may walk in his paths." The law will go out from Zion, the word of the Lord from Jerusalem. . . . They will beat their swords into plowshares and their spears into pruning hooks. Nation will not take up sword against nation, nor will they train for war anymore. "The wolf and the lamb will feed together, and the lion will eat straw like the ox." They will neither harm nor destroy on all my holy mountain, for the earth will be full of the knowledge of the Lord as the waters cover the sea (2:3, 4; 65:25; 11:9).

Sharing Your Faith

How can we as Christians effectively share our faith with the Jewish people? First, remember the differences between orthodox, conservative and reformed Jews to understand their particular religious views. Witnessing to an orthodox Jew is quite different from witnessing to a reformed Jew.

Second, use the Old Testament. This gives you common ground on which to stand.

Finally, focus on Jesus and the fact that the early believers were orthodox Jews. Christianity must always be understood as the natural outgrowth and fulfillment of God's covenant with Abraham.

During my first trip to Israel, I sat by the Jordan River with our tour guide and a guide assisting another group. The tour guide and I had talked on several occasions about Jesus. The conversation gradually shifted again to the subject of Christianity. The other guide was hostile toward any mention of Christianity. He quickly informed me that Christianity was a heretical departure from Judaism during the first century led by a radical from Nazareth named Jesus.

Earlier that morning, our group had traveled north and looked down from the mountain heights onto the Damascus Road leading from Israel into Syria. Somewhere on that road, a Pharisee named Saul of Tarsus met Jesus Christ.

So I said to the other tour guide, "If Jesus is not the Son of God risen from the dead, as multiplied thousands believed Him to be immediately after His resurrection, then explain to me Saul of Tarsus."

"What do you mean?" he asked.

I replied, "Well, Saul was a leader of orthodox Judaism. He was a Pharisee among Pharisees. He taught and lived by the strict traditions of rabbinical law. He was an enemy of the early Christians. He even went to Damascus with orders from the High Priest in Jerusalem to arrest any Jew who claimed to believe in Jesus as the promised Messiah.

"Tell me," I continued, "what happened to Saul on the Damascus Road? How do you explain such a radical turn-around in his life? He was struck down from his horse by the blinding light of the risen Lord. He was taken to a house in Damascus for three days to recover from temporary blindness. A Christian named Ananias went and prayed for him and baptized him in the name of Jesus. His sight was restored and he began preaching the gospel of Christ.

"Let's be honest," I went on, "Saul of Tarsus is the most influential Jewish rabbi who has ever lived, except for Jesus. He is also the greatest Christian missionary to carry the gospel of Christ to the world."

The Book of Acts records:

> At once he began to preach in the synagogues that Jesus is the Son of God. All those who heard him were astonished and asked, "Isn't he the man who raised havoc in Jerusalem among those who call on this name? And hasn't he come here to take them as prisoners to the chief priests?" Yet Saul grew more and more powerful and baffled the Jews living in Damascus by proving that Jesus is the Christ (9:20-22).

I then asked him, "What did Saul get for his conversion to Christ? Fame? Fortune? Power? Position? No, his conversion cost him rejection, imprisonment, suffering, loneliness and eventually a martyr's death at the order of Nero. So, we can't conclude that he had carnal, ulterior motives in becoming a Christian.

"Finally, we know from his writings in the New Testament that Saul didn't lose his mind on the Damascus Road. His writings are coherent, inspiring and enlightening. His apostolic letters like Romans, Ephesians and Philippians have transformed the course of human history."

I asked the guide again, "Now, how do you explain the dramatic change in Saul's life?"

"I can't explain it," he admitted.

I replied, "There is only one reasonable explanation for the conversion of Saul of Tarsus. It is as he said in his testimony to King Agrippa:

> I saw a light from heaven, brighter than the sun, blazing around me and my companions. We all fell to the ground and I heard a voice saying to me . . , "Saul, Saul, why do you persecute me?"
>
> Then I asked, "Who are you, Lord?"
>
> "I am Jesus whom you are persecuting," the Lord replied. "Now get up and stand on your feet. I have appeared to you to appoint you as a servant and as a witness of what you have seen of me and what I will show you" (26:13-16).

The transforming light of Christ's glory struck Saul down on Damascus Road. He looked into the face of the Son of God and his life was changed forever.

Paul gave his life for one cause: "I am not ashamed of the gospel, because it is the power of God for the salvation of everyone who believes: first for the Jew, then for the Gentile" (Romans 1:16).

Every Jew who is honestly asking, "Who is Jesus?" needs to take a look at the life of an orthodox rabbi named Saul of Tarsus who gave his life so that the world may know that Jesus is Messiah and Lord.

May the prayer of every Christian be that of Psalm 122:

I rejoiced with those who said to me, "Let us go to the house of the Lord." Our feet are standing in your gates, O Jerusalem.

Jerusalem is built like a city that is closely compacted together. That is where the tribes go up, the tribes of the Lord, to praise the name of the Lord according to the statute given to Israel. There the thrones for judgment stand, the thrones of the house of David.

Pray for the peace of Jerusalem: "May those who love you be secure. May there be peace within your walls and security within your citadels." For the sake of my brothers and friends, I will say, "Peace be within you." For the sake of the house of the Lord our God, I will seek your prosperity.

3

Is the East Really Enlightened?

A s a child of the 60s and 70s, I was a big fan of a singing group called the Beatles. I can still remember watching the Beatles perform the songs, "I Want To Hold Your Hand," and "She Loves You," on *The Ed Sullivan Show* on our black and white television.

Later, the Beatles went through a self-admitted spiritual phase. They traveled to India and studied Hinduism. Soon afterward, the sounds of the sitar, an Eastern stringed instrument, could be heard on their records. The interest in Eastern mysticism became popular in the Hippie culture and opened the way for its widespread popularity in America.

The influence of the Eastern religions in America is undeniable. Modern New Age beliefs and practices are rooted in the ancient religions of Hinduism and Buddhism.

The Eastern religions claim to offer enlightenment to their followers; an enlightenment which brings peace, tranquility and wholeness. However, is the East really enlightened?

A Hindu Temple in Atlanta?

As a native Atlantan, I was intrigued when I saw a Hindu temple being constructed on the south side of the city. I had seen many temples in India and Trinidad, but Atlanta? It shows how rapidly the world is becoming one, with the intermingling of religions and cultures.

Hinduism is one of the world's oldest religions. The essence of Hinduism is stated in the sacred writings of the Vedas: "Truth is one. They call him by different names." Hare Krishna, Christian Science and other religions derive many of their beliefs and practices from Hinduism. The word *Hinduism* comes from the Sanskrit word *Sindhu* or *Indus,* which means ocean or river.

Mahatma Gandhi said, "A man may not believe in God and still call himself a Hindu." Why did he make such a statement? He saw God as an impersonal force permeating the universe, linking all creation together as one. In Eastern philosophy, all roads can lead to God, or enlightenment, including the road of atheism.

Hinduism embraces all expressions of religion including pantheism (all is God), monotheism (one God), polytheism (many gods) and atheism (no god). Its all-inclusiveness, however, is its downfall, because it keeps the Hindu from God's true revelation of Himself in Jesus Christ.

Hinduism began in ancient India. Its primitive religious form is called the *Vedic* religion, taken from the word *Vedas,* meaning "knowledge." Worshipers sought agricultural blessings from local deities, which is characteristic of many primitive religions.

The tribes held to the notion of *animism,* a belief that everything in nature possesses a soul or spirit. This, in turn, results in the worship of everything, including animals. All the spirits are worshiped in the polytheistic religion of the Hindus. They believed that the spirits returned to earth after death in another life form. This belief is called reincarnation. Since the same life force exists in all elements of creation, whether human or animal, then the spirit could come back in any of these forms. Thus, people may return in another life as animals or insects and vice versa.

Indian history can be divided into four periods:

1. The *Pre-Vedic Period* was the time of the earliest settlers in India, who were animists.

2. The *Vedic Period* (c. 1500 B.C.) was the time of the Aryan-Indian conquerors who brought their own gods. The *Vedas,* or "wise-sayings," were written down about 1000 B.C. Polytheism developed during this time, along with the caste system.

The four major castes, from the highest to the lowest, include: *Brahmins,* priests and teachers; *Kshatriyas,* rulers and soldiers; *Vaishyas,* farmers and merchants; and *Sudras,* peasants and servants. Later, the caste system was justified on the basis of karma and reincarnation. The government of India has now officially abolished the caste system. It remains widely practiced in the villages, however.

3. The *Upanishadic Period* (c. 600 B.C.) witnessed a religious shift from the more primitive Vedic beliefs to the philosophy of the sages. They wrote the *Upanishads* articulating such beliefs as *karma,* the illusory nature of matter; *Brahman,* the Universal Soul; and *nirvana,* the final stage in reincarnation. The two theological pillars of Hinduism

are *polytheism*, the belief that God is one with creation; and *monism*, the concept that "all is one" in the universe.

4. Finally, the *Vedantic Period*, which came after Christianity, embraced the Vedantic writings as sacred writings of Hinduism. The philosopher Shankara taught that all matter is illusory, including pain and pleasure. Hinduism began to focus on self-renunciation and moral duty as a pathway to freedom and enlightenment, as well as a requirement for experiencing nirvana.[1]

Hindu Beliefs

While many Hindu sacred writings exist, the most supreme are the *Vedas* and the *Upanishads*. The most popular writing is a portion of the Indian epic, *Mahabharata,* called the *Bhagavad-Gita* meaning "the song of the Lord." The song emphasizes the importance of transcending desire, pleasure and pain.

Hinduism views God as one essence that takes on many forms or expressions. The human spirit is divine and longs for union with Brahman, the Universal Soul. This oneness with God eradicates the self. Guilt, sin and the final judgment are seen as illusory concepts. No concept of atonement or salvation is provided in Hinduism.

There does exist somewhat of a trinity, although not representative of a personal God, consisting of *Brahama,* the Creator, *Vishnu*, the Preserver, and *Shiva*, the Destroyer. The concept emerged after the dawn of Christianity and probably reflects an attempt to merge the Christian belief in the Trinity into Hinduism. My friends in India tell me that there are millions of gods in Hinduism. Everything is considered to be a god since all is connected to the Universal Soul.

While God is seen as impersonal, the concept of *avatars* developed as a compromise to the belief in a personal God. Avatars are incarnations of deity, which appear in each age to help man find his way.

The supreme avatar is the god Vishnu. Krishna, Rama and others are avatars. Partial incarnations of lesser divine forms include *swamis* (monks), *sadhus* (holy men), and *gurus* (yoga masters).

The purpose of Hinduism is to join the human soul back to the Universal Soul or the Absolute from which it came by taking one of four paths, depending on the personality of the seeker.

- The path of dedication requires devotion to a guru who is regarded as an incarnation of the divine.

- The path of service involves participation in rituals, ceremonies, pilgrimages and good works.

- The path of wisdom involves diligent study of the sacred writings and teaching by gurus and sadhus.

- The path of meditation requiring contemplation and yoga in order to discipline the mind and the body.

While Hinduism continues to gain popularity among Americans searching for enlightenment and oneness with the universe, its glaring failure to better the lives of the people in India cannot be ignored. The truth is that Hinduism has failed and is failing to deliver what it promises.

One of my close friends is Dr. Samuel Issmer. He operates a ministry in South India for orphans, street kids and children who have been discarded because of physical and mental handicaps. He grew up as a little boy in the lowest of all castes. He was told that it was his karma to live in poverty without the benefit of opportunity.

The doctrine of reincarnation had taught them that life force continues after death into the next life in either a higher or lower state, based on one's karma. Karma is the balance of good and evil deeds in one's lifetime. Good deeds lead to a higher reincarnated state of life. Evil deeds result in a lower state of life in the next life. This is the logic behind the caste system in India.

Dr. Issmer's family became Christians when he was still a young boy. In contrast to the karma teaching that it is a man's fate to remain in the condition in which he was born, Christ offers an abundant life filled with new opportunities. When he became a young man, Sam had the opportunity to attend a university in New York where he received a doctorate. Today, he serves Christ among the hurting masses in Bangalore, India.

Dr. Issmer cherishes the opportunity to share his testimony. "I came from the lowest caste," he says. "But Christ lifted me to the highest place that I may witness of His power to lift any person out of their sin and circumstances to live an abundant life."

E. Stanley Jones, a great missionary to India, tells of two Hindus traveling on a train. One man tells the other he has become a Christian.

"Why did you convert to Christianity?" the other asked. "Why do you not remain a Hindu and work to improve our religion?"

The man replied, "I don't want a religion that I can improve. I want a religion that can improve me!"

Connecting With a Hindu

The appeal of Hinduism exists partially in its all-inclusiveness. As opposed to being a well-defined system of beliefs, it incorporates into itself all religions as legitimate paths to God.

Hindus are eager to receive Jesus Christ as their Savior. I noticed this while preaching in India. Whenever I gave the invitation to receive Christ, they responded enthusiastically. They already have thousands of gods, why not add one more? The challenge is to get them to renounce all other gods and confess that Jesus Christ alone is Lord.

The Christian gospel offers lasting answers to the searching questions of Hinduism. The God who can be known is the answer to the mystery of the unknowable absolute of Hinduism. Resurrection is God's answer to the hopeless cycle of reincarnation.

God's grace provides forgiveness for the sins and is the answer to the concept of karma, which demands punishment for every evil deed. Faith, not a perfect life, is the prerequisite for heaven. Jesus, the incarnate God, is God's answer to the myth of the avatars.

Who Was Buddha?

Visit any Chinese restaurant and you will probably see a large statue of Buddha. Buddha is the founder of Buddhism. His name was Guatama (his family name) Siddhartha (his personal name). He was born in 563 B.C. in Kapilavastu, India, near Nepal. His name was changed to Buddha, meaning "enlightened one," after his experience under the famous *Bodhi* (meaning "wisdom") tree. He claimed the experience brought him enlightenment.

Buddha was born a prince and raised in the royal palace. He grew up within the confines of the palace, sheltered from the harsh realities of life. He married Princess Yasodharma when he was 16. Their son, Rahula, was born shortly afterward.

In his early 20s, he left the palace to view life outside the security he had known. For the first time in his life, he came face to face with suffering. An old man begging. People stricken with disease. A funeral procession. These encounters troubled him deeply.

According to Buddhist legend, the gods incarnated themselves in these images of suffering. He became increasingly dissatisfied with his life of excess. When he was 29, Buddha left the palace and his wife and son to search for enlightenment. For him, this meant to experience the peace of nirvana and to understand suffering.

At first he studied under two yoga masters. Then he turned to strict asceticism, subjecting himself to long fasts and self-inflicted pain. His search ended when he was 35 as he sat under a tree in a forest, where he vowed to stay until he experienced enlightenment. There he fell into a trance. While in the trance, he claimed to have remembered his previous lives.

A legend goes that Mara, the god of death, tried to discourage his efforts to find enlightenment. He sent Buddha sensual temptations, which he resisted. These were followed by life-threatening disasters. But he sat unmoved by the distractions. He reached out his hand and touched the earth, which responded with thousands upon thousands of loud roars saying, "I bear you witness."

Suddenly, enlightenment came. He claimed to be instantly free from all desires and to understand all the complex mysteries of life and suffering. Supposedly, he remained there for over 40 days in this altered state of consciousness.

He first shared his experience with five disciples in a nearby deer park. They too experienced enlightenment. For the next 49 years, Buddha traveled across India teaching his principles of enlightenment. His teachings were a reformation of Hindu beliefs. He challenged the practices of Hinduism, particularly the order of the Brahmin priests for their detachment from common people. He also questioned the authority of the Vedic writings, and called for the abolishment of the caste system.

What Buddha Believed

Buddha rejected the notions of absolute reality, the concept of God, the existence of good and evil, and the reality of the human soul. His teachings represented something of a middle-of-the-road approach between asceticism and the indulgence of desires.

He maintained the Hindu beliefs in reincarnation, karma and nirvana. The word *nirvana*, means "to blow out," and was defined by Buddha as a state of bliss in which one is free from all desires. Buddha taught that suffering results from man's desire for pleasure. The way to end suffering is to extinguish all desires. He taught an eight-fold path to enlightenment.[2]

1. *Right Beliefs.* Followers are taught the Four Noble Truths: existence involves suffering, suffering results from desires for pleasure, extinguishing desire ends suffering, and suffering is ended by following the eight-fold path.

2. *Right Motives.* Enlightenment involves maintaining pure motives in one's actions and relationships.

3. *Right Speech.* The enlightened person practices truthful and beneficial communication

4. *Right Conduct.* Buddha developed his own version of the ten commandments: (1) You shall not kill any living creature. (2) You shall not take what is not yours. (3) You shall not commit adultery. (4) You shall not lie, but speak the word of truth. (5) You shall not partake of intoxicating liquors. (6) You shall not partake of food after midday. (7) You shall not attend any drama, dance or musical performance. (8) You shall not use any personal adornment or perfume. (9) You shall not sleep on a broad, comfortable bed. (10) You shall not own any gold or silver.

5. *Right Vocation.* One's work must always promote life and never harm anyone.

6. *Right Effort.* The enlightened person is determined to live by the Four Noble Truths.

7. *Right Thinking.* One must have control of thoughts for self-examination.

8. *Right Focus.* Enlightenment is achieved only through meditation and yoga.

Buddha placed man at the center of the universe and gave no attention to the origin of humanity. He claimed that ignorance, not sin, is the problem of humanity and causes all suffering. Concepts such as heaven and hell, as well as a belief about the end of the world, are nonexistent in Buddhism. We are to look inward to discover the Buddha within us all, not upward to God for enlightenment and truth.

Buddhists believe man has no soul but that he exists only in body, emotions, ideas, will and pure consciousness. Nirvana, the state of perfect enlightenment, can only be achieved through successive transmigrations in reincarnated states based on one's karma. Such complete awareness frees one from all feeling, including hate and love.

Buddha died at the age of 80 (c. 480 B.C.). After his death, his teachings were expanded by his followers and continue to spread across the Orient and to the Mideast, including Israel and Egypt. By the third century A.D., Buddhism had moved into the Far East, and by the sixth and seventh centuries, came to Japan and Tibet. Today, Buddhism has been imported by the West, which seems preoccupied with the eastern religions in its search for enlightenment.

Variations on a Theme

America has been invaded by two forms of Buddhism: *Tibetan Buddhism* and *Zen-Buddhism*. Tibetan Buddhism began in A.D. 747 as a blend of sorcery and Buddhism under a pagan exorcist named Padina Sambhava. Religious practices involve spells, secretive rituals, and the use of mantras and mandalas (circular cosmograms of the universe).

They developed the concept of *Shambhala*, a kingdom of enlightened ones. Their *Book of the Dead* speaks of demons, spirits and powers of witchcraft, which must be both avoided and appeased.

In 1951 Communist soldiers invaded the Tibetan kingdom. The Dalai Lama, who was worshiped by his followers as a god-king, fled from the Chinese in 1959 with 110,000 refugees and settled in India. He has toured the West, including the United States, and has been hailed as a great spiritual leader by some ecumenical religious leaders.

Zen-Buddhism has become the most popular and widespread form of Buddhism in the West. The founder of Zen is Bodhidharma, who studied Buddhism in India for 40 years and then returned to China. He sat in a cave for nine years staring at a wall. His legs atrophied and he cut off his eyelids to sustain open-eye meditation.

Zen focuses on *koans*, which are paradoxical questions such as: "If a tree falls in the woods, and there is no one present to hear it, does it make a sound?" The goal of *koans* is to cause the mind to think beyond the boundaries of logic and reason, which are considered taboo, in order to experience intuitive truth.

Zen denies dualism of any form including good and evil, time and space, present and future. All that exists is what man conceives. Objective reality is an illusion, according to Zen.

While traditional Buddhism offers enlightenment after several reincarnated lives, Zen promises enlightenment to its followers, here-and-now. This fast-track path to enlightenment is especially appealing to Westerners. Zen focuses on meditation, designed to empty the mind of all earthly thoughts and give the seeker a sense of peace and oneness with all things.[3]

Connecting With Buddhists

Buddhism is being popularized in the United States because it focuses on the self; it requires no obedience to a higher authority, including God; and it defines truth as personal experience. The spiritual vacuum evident among many Americans today is being partially filled by Eastern mysticism.

The Christian gospel offers both Hindus and Buddhists the joy of knowing God personally and experiencing true revelation from the Holy Spirit and from the Scripture. The problem with humanity is not ignorance, and the solution is not enlightenment. The problem is sin and the solution is forgiveness and salvation through Jesus Christ.

We do not lack fulfillment because we are unenlightened. We lack fulfillment because we are separated from God. Jesus bridged the gap between man and God caused by sin. He alone has the power to reconcile us to God. Fulfillment does not come by emptying the mind. It comes when we are filled with the fullness of God. The early disciples were "filled with joy and with the Holy Spirit" (Acts 13:52). While Buddhists seek to empty their lives of pain and pleasure, Christians seek the fullness of goodness and grace of God so that we can truly say, "My cup runs over!"

The East remains in spiritual darkness. Enlightenment comes only from God, who has revealed Himself in His Son Jesus Christ. The only enlightenment a Hindu or a Buddhist needs is the understanding of God's love and His eternal plan of salvation in Jesus Christ.

Paul offers a powerful prayer of enlightenment:

> I keep asking that the God of our Lord Jesus Christ, the glorious Father, may give you the Spirit of wisdom and revelation, so that you may know him better. I pray also that the eyes of your heart may be enlightened in order that you may know the hope to which he has called you, the riches of his glorious inheritance in the saints, and his incomparably great power for us who believe (Ephesians 1:17-19).

As a young pastor, I led my first mission trip to Trinidad. Our group traveled into the central mountain range to a village named Penal. I was scheduled to speak at an evening service being held in a church, which was a former Hindu temple. Before his conversion to Christ, the pastor had served as a Hindu priest in that temple.

After he began preaching the gospel of Christ, he was opposed vigorously by militant Hindus. His life had been threatened on several occasions. He had endured severe harassment. Still, he persevered in his ministry. His Christian name was George, and he enjoyed wearing a big cowboy hat. He was quite a character.

After the service concluded, my group and I went to his home located next to the church. While we were having dessert, I said to him, "George, tell me how you came from being a Hindu priest for 25 years to become a Christian and a minister of the gospel. Did missionaries come to Penal and lead you to Christ? How did you first hear the gospel?"

He replied, "No one came and preached the gospel."

"How, then, did you hear about Jesus Christ?" I asked.

He handed me a Hindu book and turned to a page with a sentence in the middle of the page. "Do you recognize that statement?" he asked with a big smile.

"Of course I do," I replied. To my amazement there were the words of John 1:14 concerning the incarnation of Jesus, "The Word was made flesh, and dwelt among us, (and we beheld his glory, the glory as of the only begotten of the Father,) full of grace and truth" (KJV).

He said, "One day I was reading this Hindu book and came upon this statement. So, I prayed to God, 'Who is the Word that was made flesh?' I pondered the meaning of this statement and sought enlightenment."

He continued, "One night I had a dream. Jesus Christ suddenly appeared to me. He revealed Himself to me as Lord. I dreamed that I was a little baby again, and that I was being dipped into a pool of water and then lifted out of the water. I knew it was a dream of new life. When I awoke I gave my life to Jesus Christ and vowed to serve Him. I began reading the Bible and started to preach the gospel to my people."

This man has since led hundreds to know Christ as Lord in Penal, in spite of being persecuted. A former Hindu temple is now a Christian church all because one Hindu priest found true enlightenment in one sentence from the Gospel of John and asked God for enlightenment.

Truly, God is the missionary. We are simply instruments in His hand when we share our faith. God reveals Himself to everyone who seeks Him. Revelation comes from God to every human heart that will listen to His voice and believe the gospel.

4

What's New About New Age?

oday we hear a lot of talk about the New Age. Bookstores offer a venue of New Age literature, which deals with everything from self-help and spirituality to extraterrestrial travel and spirit possession. Music stores provide a genre of New Age music. Even politicians speak of a new world order.

What is the New Age movement? The term conjures up images of Shirley MacLaine, channelers, crystals, psychics and astrologers. The New Age movement represents a blending of religious beliefs and occultic practices under one umbrella. Carl A. Raschke, professor of religious studies at the University of Denver, says, "The New Age movement is essentially the maturing of the hippie movement of the 1960s."

Robert Lindsay, of the *New York Times,* puts the New Age into perspective: "According to experts in sociology, religion and psychology . . . the phenomenon is less a movement than a collection of disparate organizations and iconoclasts challenging orthodox thinking in a wide range of subjects, from religion to physics." New Age thought, according to many proponents as well as detractors, directly or indirectly rejects the Judeo-Christian concept of a single, omnipotent God who has revealed His will to humanity. Instead, New Age adherents follow the view of many eastern religions that there is a unity in the universe, of which all things, including God and man, are equal parts.[1]

J. Gordon Melton, director of the Institute for the Study of American Religion in Santa Barbara, California, points out that "since the mid-1960s, there has been a steady increase in openness to metaphysical and occultic ideas in the United States. Beliefs that have existed for a long time on the metaphysical periphery are now becoming very much part of Middle America."[2]

Fergus M. Bordewich says, "New Age philosophy is becoming the religion, or at least the ethos, of a growing proportion of the young, professional middle class that is now beginning to move into positions of responsibility and authority in American society."[3]

NEW AGE BELIEFS

The Nature of God

Scripture reveals one God who is Creator, Redeemer and Father. God is the ultimate reality, the Absolute of the universe. Atheism presupposes that God does not exist, suggesting that the universe came into being by naturalistic causes and evolutionary processes. Religion is considered by the New Age to be an invention of the unenlightened human mind.

Pantheism is the belief that God and the world are essentially the same. God is not a personal being but is rather the impersonal cosmic power (laws and forces), which binds the universe together as one.

The earth and all its forces are called "God." We are God and God is us. The goal of pantheism is to achieve oneness with the universe, or the forces of nature; to live in harmony with nature. Evil and good are myths; there is only order and chaos. The loss of oneness results in chaos. Reality is not absolute or objective; man creates his own reality.

Pantheism, as is true of the eastern religions, is the underlying theology of New Ageism.

Life After Death

New Agers believe that nothing happens after death because no reality exists outside the world of space, time and matter. New Agers also believe in reincarnation, and view death as a passage into unending life cycles. Only perfection can free a person from the unending cycle and lead to nirvana, which is loosely defined as one's absorption into eternal reality.

The cycle is governed by *karma*—the process of action and reaction or the cosmic law of cause and effect, which states that everyone receives what he or she deserves. One's karma, the sum total of his bad and good deeds, determines the quality of life he enjoys during his next reincarnated life cycle.

Morality

Christians believe that morals and ethics are rooted in the revelation of God and His law as found in the Bible.

Moral relativism runs contrary to the Christian view asserting that moral decisions rest on situations and personal desires. New Ageism holds to an optimistic, and I might add unrealistic, view of human nature rejecting the validity of sin and guilt. This would also exclude the need for divine forgiveness and redemption.

Blaise Pascal, the French scientist noted that, "In a values vacuum, humanity will pursue one of two goals: We will imagine that we ourselves are god or we will seek gratification through our senses." New Ageism in America has driven us in both directions simultaneously.

Acquiring Knowledge

Learning begins with reason. Science is the process of attaining knowledge through observation, experimentation and organization of data. But knowledge can also be gained through spiritual revelation. God not only reveals Himself through objective reality, but also through the ministry of the Holy Spirit as He speaks to the human soul.

Like eastern mysticism, the New Age promises hidden and secret knowledge to followers, which can be attained through altered states of consciousness. Altered states, ranging from intense concentration to ecstatic trances, are achieved through transcendental meditation, astral projection, contact with spirit guides and ascended masters, centering, yoga, imaging (visualization), channeling, psychic experiences and drug use.

Knowledge is the key to oneness with the universe. Those without knowledge still see themselves as individuals, as opposed to being part of the cosmic whole. Not having yet recognized their divinity, they see life only as fragmented events, as opposed to part of an overall master plan into which all the events fit. Reason and belief stand as enemies to enlightenment and need to be eliminated.

Jesus and the New Age

The New Age views Jesus as an ascended master. He is one who achieved oneness with ultimate reality like Buddha, Krishna, Elijah, Mohammed, Alexander the Great and others. According to the New Age, Jesus is but one of many avatars, who are persons sent to show us the way to enlightenment.

The "Christ Event" represents the moment He achieved godhood and was absorbed back into the ultimate reality of the universe. He was not "the Christ" but "a Christ." He realized His inherent divinity—a realization everyone needs to experience. Every person has the potential for Christhood in New Ageism.

New Agers stress the importance of self-esteem, which means the realization of our own inherent divinity. They agree with German mystic Meister Johannes Eckhart (1260-1328) who wrote a meditation which reads:

> The Lord of love, immortal and infinite, comes as a divine incarnation in times of great crisis to rescue mankind from disaster. Sri Krishna, the Compassionate Buddha, and Jesus the Christ are supreme examples.[4]

The New Age denies Jesus of His own uniqueness as the Son of God, the Savior of the world, and the King of kings who possesses all authority both in heaven and on earth. The New Age sees the final evolution of human society into the cosmic Christ as the second coming of Christ. Man, not God—they say—will create this utopia called "the Age of Aquarius" through his own enlightenment.

Views of Sin

Sin is a universal problem. "All have sinned and fall short of the glory of God" (Romans 3:23). Sin is both a state of living and an action of rebellion against God and His Word. Why is there evil in the world? Why is there suffering, war, poverty, crime and death, if God made the world and declared it good? Did God create evil? Even worse, is He both good and evil?

Only the Book of Genesis explains and accounts for the universal presence of sin in the world. There are two sources of sin. First, the tempter, called Satan or the devil, promised Adam and Eve that they could be like God with complete knowledge.

Second, sin comes from human choice. God placed Adam and Eve in Eden to care for it. He told them, "You are free to eat from any tree in the garden; but you must not eat from the tree of the knowledge of good and evil, for when you eat of it you will surely die" (2:16, 17).

The Hebrew words for good and evil are *tob* and *ra,* meaning the pleasure and the pain. The issue was one of trust. Would they trust God's wisdom or go their own way? This is the essence of sin: we reject God's way to go our own way.

The Fall narrative refutes evolution. Instead of starting at the bottom and evolving to the top, we started at the top and fell to the bottom. Second, the Fall refutes humanism. Humanism asserts that man is basically good. The environment conditions him to be bad. The fact is, man was tested in a perfect environment.

Third, the Fall teaches that humankind is responsible. We are subject to God and accountable to Him. The command, "You shall not eat it," underscores humanity's dependency on God for morality and truth. We are responsible to God for our moral choices.

The concept of sin presupposes an absolute authority, which is transgressed. The New Age says evil is an illusion. Since no moral absolute exists, sin cannot exist. This being the case, man does not need a redeemer because he is not a sinner.

Sin is an act of resisting God's will, rejecting God's Word, and departing from God's way, either consciously or unconsciously. The only antidote for sin is the forgiveness of God. We are "justified freely by his grace through the redemption that came by Christ Jesus" (Romans 3:24).

Distinctive Features

Certain features of the New Age make it easily identifiable. First, the god of the new age is an impersonal force within all creation. God is all, and all is god.

Second, man is god who creates the force of life. He only needs to awaken the creative powers residing within him by which he can achieve his highest potential and create a social utopia.

Third, man should seek and accept spiritual enlightenment directly from the spirit world through the process of altered states of consciousness. Contact with the dead and with spirit guides is sought.

Fourth, all religions have equal merit; they all lead to God, or enlightenment. While New Ageism borrows heavily from Christian terminology, it distorts the true meaning of Christian beliefs.

Fifth, the ancient wisdom of Babylon, Egypt and Greece—not the Bible—provides the basis of truth for New Ageism. The highest virtue is what feels right. This leads to moral relativism as seen in the Book of Judges —"everyone did as he saw fit" (Judges 21:25).

Sixth, New Ageism parts company with both Christianity and science. Its validation of mystical and magical experiences casts a shadow of doubt over rational thought. Its denial of the past as a basis for action separates people from both their own and society's history. The New Age elevates fables over objective reality.

Seventh, New Ageism seeks to influence political, social, educational, economic and religious institutions. It is associated with the human potential movement in humanistic psychology, holistic health, astrology, channeling, deep ecology (which rejects the view that nature exists to serve humanity), feminism (goddess worship) and parapsychology (ESP, psychic phenomena and out-of-body experiences). Some major corporations offer New Age workshops designed to help employees handle stress, develop healthier relationships and increase productivity.

Eighth, metaphysical techniques including yoga, meditation, releasing, centering and crystals are used to combat illness, manage stress and achieve happiness. What we think, we become. We create our own reality through higher levels of consciousness.

Ninth, New Ageism travels with the occult. It uses crystals, Tarot cards, Ouija boards and witchcraft. Witchcraft, commonly known as Wicca, is presented falsely as a positive force for social change, detaching itself openly from such concepts of Satanism.

Tenth, New Ageism emphasizes globalism and the dethronement of national sovereignty. The concept of oneness has political implications, which sets the stage for the globalization of economy, government, military, police force and religion.

The New Age is really nothing more than a new version of an old lie. Satan told Adam and Eve, that if they were to disobey God, their eyes would be opened and they would be like God, knowing good from evil (Genesis 3:5).

The New Age has a strong appeal because of its denial of original sin and human guilt, its elevation of humanity to a place of divinity, its freedom from responsibility to God and others, and its empowerment of people with feelings of superiority.

Scientology and Hollywood

Our discussion of cults and New Ageism would be incomplete without a brief look at a cult gaining prominence in America called Scientology. The cult is gaining popularity in Hollywood among some noted actors. Scientology is part science fiction and part self-help.

During the 70s, you were likely to be met on the street of a metropolitan city by a strangely clad individual called a Hare Krishna. Today you're more apt to meet a well-dressed man or woman offering you a free "personality assessment." Their 200-question survey is actually a recruitment method for the Church of Scientology. The name even sounds catchy, but it is far from being scientific.

Scientology has been labeled one of the most dangerous cults of our day. It claims to be an applied religious
philosophy that offers a "clear, bright insight to help you
blaze towards your mind's full potential." Its technique of
dianetics (meaning "through the soul") promises to
reveal "the single source of all man's insanities, psycho-
somatic illnesses and neuroses." Scientology uses a
strange nomenclature. They have published their own
dictionary containing over 7,000 words.

Scientology was founded in 1955 by L. Ron Hubbard
(1911-1986) in Washington, D.C. The guru-like leader over-
saw all Scientology activities from an offshore fleet of ships.
His first book, *Dianetics: The Modern Science of Mental
Health,* published in 1950, has sold more than 15 million
copies. The book sets forth Hubbard's psychotherapeutic
answer to the failed practices of traditional psychiatry.

Hubbard and his contemporaries launched an all-out
attack against psychiatry. The medical community reacted
with alarm and investigated his claims. In 1971, a Federal
Court ruled that Hubbard's medical claims were bogus. He
countered by seeking refuge through registering Scientology as an official religion with tax-exempt status and
freedom from governmental influence for some of his
organizations.

Hubbard said that humans are made of clusters of spirits (*thetans*) banished to earth 75 million years ago by a
cruel galactic ruler named Xenu. He claimed that humans
descended from a race of gods, called *thetans,* who forfeited their power to enter Material-Energy-Space-Time
(mest) world of earth. Over time, however, they evolved
through reincarnation into humans who could no longer

remember their divine existence. Humans, then, are gods who don't know they are gods.

The goal of Scientology is to help humans rediscover their godhood, or dormant *thetan* potential, by removing all mental blocks, called *engrams,* along with emotional barriers and repressed memories stored in the unconscious. As persons realize their divinity, they will achieve power over and freedom from *mest.*

Engrams are defined as traumatic memories from past lives. A new recruit, called a PC for *preclear,* goes through a therapeutic process to clear the engrams from the mind. This is done by use of an E-Meter, which is said to measure resistance to electricity by reading galvanic skin responses. As with a polygraph, the interviewer, called an *auditor*, asks a series of questions while the respondent holds the E-Meter in his hands. Scientologists liken this process to a confessional and claim that a person can be *clear* of the psychic hindrances of their engrams.

Practicing Scientology is very expensive for its followers, which has, in turn, produced a very lucrative enterprise for Scientology. Persons have been plunged into financial ruin after the church has exhausted all of their financial resources.

While the movement has sought to gain mainstream acceptance by promoting its anti-drug abuse program called Narconon®, abstinence from premarital sex and adultery, and efforts with prisoners and the mentally handicapped, the dangers of the cult are well documented. Complaints have been made against the church for harassment, intimidation and defamation of critics.

A major creed of Scientology as espoused by L. Ron Hubbard is that "man is good." Man's innate goodness is based on the view that man is a fallen god seeking to evolve to reclaim his divinity as a *thetan*. Dianetics advocates such practices as astral travel and regression into past lives, which are based on reincarnation. Hubbard claimed that his teachings were the path to spiritual freedom and the spiritual heir of Buddhism in the Western world.[5]

While Scientologists seek fulfillment in a past life, Jesus Christ promises an abundant life today and forever. While they claim to be able to clear the mind, Jesus promises to cleanse and forgive our sins and to reconcile humanity to God.

During the early 1970s, the IRS proved that Hubbard was taking millions of dollars from the church, laundering money through a false corporation in Panama and stashing it in Swiss bank accounts. Eleven top Scientologists, including Hubbard's third wife, went to prison in the early 1980s for infiltrating, burglarizing and wiretapping over a hundred private and government agencies in attempts to block their investigations. In 1985, the IRS was seeking an indictment of Hubbard for tax fraud. He remained in hiding for five years and died in 1986 before the criminal case could be prosecuted. High-level defectors say the organization has stashed away hundreds of millions of dollars in foreign bank accounts.

Why do people get trapped in such an obvious and dangerous cult? Some are attracted to the promise of mental and physical well-being, especially if they have been disappointed by traditional psychiatry. The emphasis on the goodness of human nature and the prospects of rediscovering past lives and achieving divinity have a

strong appeal to many who have turned away from orthodox beliefs.

All this nonsense about being gods, reminds us of
Satan's lie to Adam and Eve, when he tempted them to disobey God. "'You will not surely die,' the serpent said to the
woman. 'For God knows that when you eat of it your eyes
will be opened, and you will be like God'" (Genesis 3:4, 5).
It was a lie then, and it is still a lie. It is better by far to trust
God and to worship Him, than to try to become Him.

Let me share with you the personal story of someone
I know who became confused by Scientology and found
her way out. She wrote me the following letter:

> My exposure to Scientology began in a rather unassuming
> way. It came through a business/consulting group. This
> group, an organization called WISE, began its consulting
> with a little hint of broader intentions. Gradually, as the
> consulting began to be working for the business, the arena
> of "solutions" began to broaden. I found myself taking
> extensive high level courses at the local Scientology center.
>
> As I finished one of the courses, the staff began talking to
> me about my life and were there any problems or concerns
> that needed to be handled. My marriage was already a big
> question mark for me, so the promises and opportunities
> were especially inviting. After a few relationship courses,
> they hit me with the "big guns." What I really needed was
> "auditing." The purpose of this was to remove what are
> called engrams from your subconscious.
>
> Scientology believes that we have all lived many lives,
> in many places and planets, and that when bad and
> painful things happen to us, they become stuck in our

minds and are the source of our problems today. So the only way to handle today's problems is through auditing. The result is a "clear mind." I spent close to eight weeks at a Scientology center in Washington, D.C. doing nothing but auditing every day, from morning 'til night.

Well, I'm clear! Do I feel different? No! It's done, and that alone feels good. But wait—now there is a whole new series of auditing I must do to get all my abilities back. I'm in danger. Now my head is spinning. Will there ever be an end? Will I ever get to that promise of total freedom? Is Scientology the "only hope for all mankind" as they taught?

While all this training had been going on, my husband (we were now divorced) became increasingly concerned for my well-being and began to learn all he could about Scientology. The more he learned, the greater his concern became. He contacted a Christian group called Watchman Fellowship, whose purpose was to help people who were in cults get out. They spent an entire Sunday with me, lovingly trying to open my eyes. Though I didn't want my eyes opened, seeds were planted and I give thanks every day for these dedicated and caring people, and my husband, because what they did for me that day made a huge difference in my life!

The very next course I took in Scientology (there is always a next course) had to do with gathering all the information on both sides of an issue in working toward a solution. Well, I walked up to the instructor and said, "I've always called myself a Christian and you say I can be a Christian and a Scientologist. I really don't know what being a Christian means. I need more information. Goodbye!"

I was out the door before he could say a word and I've never gone back—thank God! God reconciled my marriage and brought me into a personal relationship with Him where I finally found total freedom and it didn't cost me a penny. I can't begin to explain the joy and peace in my life now. Some people might think that I probably feel pretty stupid to be involved in such a cult, but I just feel grateful that God brought me out. Anyone is susceptible, especially if he or she doesn't know our mighty and awesome God!

From New Age to New Birth

A testimony from Sharon Beekman reveals the dangers of the New Age and confirms the liberty of knowing Jesus as Lord.

The evil within and around me manipulated my body, emotions and thoughts, much as a cat playing with a half-dead mouse. The problem had started in 1977, when I began exploring psychic phenomena and the spiritual realm. In a meditation class at a spiritualist church, I learned to be a channel for spirits. I also studied the I-Ching, acupressure, Tarot, Native American and Eastern spirituality, astrology and the Seth books. I established a ritual of yoga and meditation an hour each morning.

By 1985 I had difficulty completing thoughts. I lacked emotion and lived in isolation. I was a poor reflection of the vibrant, successful mental health professional I once had been.

I decided to stop channeling. It was then the spirits revealed their true nature. I called Tad, a Christian friend from college, and described my situation. My harassment worsened after I received the materials from Tad. Finally, one night I sobbed, "I've got to find a Christian . . . I need Jesus Christ."

In the spring of 1987, acting on Tad's advice, I called an inner-city church. "I'm demon- possessed," I said, "and would like to know Jesus Christ. Could someone there help me?"

Without hesitating, the church secretary said, "Yes, we would love to talk with you. Come right down!"

After introductions, the young pastor and a woman from the congregation bowed their heads and prayed. They sounded like children appealing to a loving father. Their love for God impressed me. I longed to love in that way.

As the pastor described God's love for me, the spirits screamed objections in my mind. But I knew they lied. "What do I need to do?" I asked. "Well, Sharon, Romans 10:9 says if you confess with your mouth, that Jesus is Lord, and believe in your heart that God raised him from the dead, you will be saved."

Eagerly I prayed aloud, "Lord Jesus Christ, I confess that I have sinned against you. Please forgive me. I want You to be Lord and Savior of my life. Amen." As they continued praying, I felt the Spirit of God fill the cold place at my center.

Every week for the next year I attended church services, participated in a Bible study, and prayed with the pastor and a lay minister. I also emptied my house of all paraphernalia associated with the occult and New Age thinking.

I called my friend Tad. "Jesus quieted my mind," I told her, "but do you know the greatest miracle of all? He's changing me! That sense of emptiness is gone and I feel loved, really loved, and I genuinely love others. What a miracle!"[6]

5

Stars, Cards and Psychics

U.S. News & World Report poll found that nearly 60 percent of Americans think the world will end sometime in the future and almost a third of those think it will end within a few decades. More than 61 percent say they believe in the second coming of Christ. Nearly half believe a literal Antichrist will arise and 44 percent believe a battle of Armageddon will occur.[1]

People are not only interested in Bible prophecy, they're interested in their personal future. A preoccupation with knowing the future has resulted in a renewed interest in astrology and psychic phenomena. Astrology is an occult practice in the same category as fortune-telling, palmistry, Tarot cards, witchcraft (often called Wicca), numerology, spiritism, magic and necromancy (contacting the dead). Interestingly, the resurgence of the occult parallels the boom of science and technology.

Many Americans were shocked in 1988 when Nancy Reagan consulted an astrologer to influence her husband, then President Ronald Reagan, in his political decisions. According to the *Atlanta Journal-Constitution* (December 3, 1994), 20 percent of Americans believe in astrology and 90 percent of all newspapers carry the horoscope.

Searching the Stars

Astrology has been widely denounced by astronomers and scientists as superstitious and unfounded. Yet, many people hold to the belief that astrology works. Apparently, they find a measure of consolation offered by the horoscope. Instead of reading the Scripture every morning to hear from God, people choose to read their horoscope.

Astrology has been around since the days of the ancient Babylonians—at least 5,000 years ago. They believed the planets were gods whose movements in the heavens influenced the destinies of men. Since such earlier methods of predicting the future, like examining the entrails of animals, proved unreliable, they relied on the predictable movements of the stars.

Astrology is the art of forecasting the future and interpreting the influence celestial bodies have on the destinies of humans. Astrology differs from astronomy, which is the science of the celestial bodies including their motions, magnitudes, distances and physical constitution.

The word *horoscope* comes from the Greek language and means, "to observe the time." The *zodiac* is an imaginary belt or path in the heavens that the sun and the principal planets travel as they circle the earth. The zodiac consists of 12 constellations or signs, called *houses*, which form a circular path around the earth. Of course, we know, the sun and the planets do not travel around the earth.

The 12 constellations, or signs of the zodiac, move through each house during a year. The nine planets, along with the sun and moon, move through the houses every 24 hours. Astrological readings are based on the assumed dates that the sun enters each house. Astrologers are concerned with the time certain star constellations appear in the pathway of the sun as its rays pass through the constellation to the earth.

In addition to the 12 signs, there are 36 *decans*, meaning "pieces." There are three decans per house to complement the 12 signs. For example, the sign Aries, the Lamb, also has the decans, Cassiopeia, the Enthroned Woman; Cetus, the Sea-Monster; and Perseus, the Breaker.

Where did these signs come from? No one knows for sure. No matter how far back we go in antiquity, they are always there. The ancients used the signs to describe something that happened prior to their day.

The zodiac is used to make predictions about the future and to determine one's destiny. The 12 signs of the zodiac correspond with the 12 months of the year. People born under certain signs are supposed to have distinct personalities. Shakespeare described Romeo and Juliet as star-crossed lovers who were destined for tragedy because of the stars under which they were born. Lovers today still consult the zodiac to see if their signs are compatible.

Nearly all cultures have the same 12 signs, although archaeologists and historians have yet to discover why the same signs exists in so many cultures. Interestingly, the constellations, which represent the 12 signs of the zodiac, bear absolutely no resemblance to the pictures of the signs themselves. The Big Dipper, called Ursa Major (the Great Bear), doesn't look anything like a bear.

Astrology is a fallible system. It simply does not reveal the future or one's personal destiny. The ancient Babylonians, or Chaldeans, who devised astrology and the Romans who practiced it, believed the universe circled around the earth. Copernicus proved that theory wrong. The ancients also thought that there were only five planets, since only five can be seen by the naked eye—Mercury, Venus, Mars, Jupiter and Saturn. They included the sun and moon to arrive at the perfect number, seven. Since the pre-Copernican concept of the earth being at the center of the universe is wrong, so is the zodiac.

One's horoscope is determined by calculating the geographical location and time of birth in conjunction with the position of the constellations. But since the horoscope is based on the fallacy that the earth is the center of the universe, all such calculations are completely false. This, however, doesn't seem to matter to those who follow their horoscope, who are more concerned with myth than reality.[2]

Some people are born without a horoscope. Eskimos and Norwegians born north of the Arctic Circle go without seeing a single planet of the zodiac for weeks. So, they are left without the stars and planets to influence their destinies.

What about twins? They are born at the same time and place. Should not their personalities and destinies be similar since they are born under the same sign? But we all know that twins are distinct individuals. Also, there are many other constellations which are not included in the zodiac. Why do these constellations have no influence on us? Astrology cannot answer these challenging questions.

The precession of the equinoxes disproves astrology. The earth is tilting slightly on its equinox, which has caused the zodiac to shift over time. Today, the rays of the sun enter each of the constellations at least a month earlier than they did when the present astrological charts were developed. The characteristics of each zodiac sign no longer apply to the months to which they have been assigned. The constellations supposed to inhabit the 12 houses aren't even there anymore.[3]

Astrology is practiced universally, yet no two religions agree on the interpretations of the zodiac. A horoscope read by a Hindu in India would be interpreted quite differently if read by a Buddhist in China.

Horoscopes differ on the personality descriptions of Aries, Pisces, Libra and so forth. The fact is, horoscope readings and the description of an individual's sign are so vague and general they could describe anyone on any given day of the week. People want to believe that their lives possess some mystical destiny. The need to feel significant causes people to convince themselves that the horoscope is accurate. They read what they want to read into their horoscope.

Astrology in the Bible

The Bible is far from silent on the subject of astrology. It reveals the futility of astrology and condemns its practices. Astrologers often refer to Biblical passages, which reference the constellations to support their beliefs. The references, however, do not support astrology but rather teach the sovereignty of God over creation, including the planets and the stars.

God created the stars as "signs to mark seasons and days and years" (Genesis 1:14). Astrology is a distortion of God's revelation of Himself and the plan of salvation as told in the story of the stars. Paul the apostle says that Creation is the first and primary revelation of God. "For since the creation of the world God's invisible qualities—his eternal power and his divine nature—have been clearly seen, being understood from what has been made, so that men are without excuse" (Romans 1:20).

The ancients attested to the glory of God revealed in the heavens. "He is the Maker of the Bear and Orion, the Pleiades and the constellations of the south" (Job 9:9). The prophet Amos says, "Seek the Lord and live . . . he who made the Pleiades and Orion . . . the Lord is his name" (5:6, 8). In Job we read, "By his breath the skies became fair; his hand pierced the gliding serpent," a reference to the Crooked Serpent, one of the greatest constellations (26:13).

God arranged the stars in their places and gave them their significance. From the earliest of times, these stars and signs have been known. Astronomers can know when a past event took place by the changing and shifting of the stars. According to Arabic tradition, the signs came from Seth and Enoch, the son and grandson of Adam. But the ancient astrologers corrupted the meaning of the signs as seen in the tower of Babel.[4]

The Book of Job records a fascinating dialogue between God and his servant Job. As God reveals His sovereignty over Creation, He asks: "Can you bind the beautiful Pleiades? Can you loose the cords of Orion? Can you bring forth the constellations in their seasons or lead out the Bear [or Leo] with its cubs? Do you know the laws of the heavens? Can you set up [God's] dominion over the earth?" (38:31-33).

Here are direct Biblical references to the constellations of Orion and Pleiades, and the star Arcturus (the Bear). The names of these heavenly bodies appear in what is considered to be the oldest book in the Bible. The Book of Job is dated c. 2150 B.C., which would make Job a contemporary of Abraham.

God condemns the practice of astrology. The first Biblical reference to astrology appears in Genesis 11 with the account of building of the tower of Babel. *Babel* is the root of the word *Babylon* and means "confusion." The famed tower was not a tower to reach heaven, as though the builders were trying to reach God. The ill-fated tower was an ancient ziggurat, many of which have been excavated in Mesopotamia, and served as a platform by which to observed the stars. Many of the excavated ziggurats display the various signs of the zodiac on their upper levels.

What really happened at Babel? The heavenly signs, which told the story of God's grace and called humankind to worship Him, were corrupted into pagan deities. People began worshiping the stars, the sun and moon, and the planets instead of the God who created them. Isaiah condemned the practice of astrology.

All the counsel you have received has only worn you out! Let your astrologers come forward, those stargazers who make predictions month by month, let them save you from what is coming upon you. Surely they are like stubble; the fire will burn them up. They cannot even save themselves from the power of the flame. Here are no coals to warm anyone; here is no fire to sit by. That is all they can do for you—these you have labored with and trafficked with since childhood. Each of them goes on in his error; there is not one that can save you (47:13-15).

Jeremiah denounced astrology, which was prevalent in the Babylonian culture. "Do not learn the ways of the nations or be terrified by signs in the sky" (Jeremiah 10:2). What a tragedy when people worship "created things rather than the Creator—who is forever praised" (Romans 1:25).

The impotence of astrologers, psychics and fortune-tellers is clearly portrayed in the Book of Daniel. One night Nebuchadnezzar, the king of Babylon, had a disturbing dream. He called an emergency meeting with his "magicians, enchanters, sorcerers and astrologers" (2:2). He wanted them to recount his dream and then interpret it. But none of them could.

Daniel was then summoned to assist the king. But he did not use the occult. Daniel requested time to pray that God would reveal the dream and its meaning to him. He would then inform the king. His request was granted.

After Daniel and his friends prayed, he went to the king and told him: "No wise man, enchanter, magician or diviner can explain to the king the mystery he has asked about, *but there is a God in heaven who reveals mysteries.* He has shown King Nebuchadnezzar what will happen in days to come" (vv. 27, 28, emphasis added).

He revealed the dream and its meaning to the king. It foretold the coming of successive world empires, beginning with Babylon and ending with Rome. The account underscores two truths. First, astrology has no ability to reveal the future, because it is a fallible system. Second, only God can reveal the future, which He does only to show what He is doing in the world.

The impotency of astrology is underscored in the Book of Revelation. John sees the New Jerusalem in eternity. The city is built on 12 foundations made of precious stones (see 21:19, 20). The stones of the foundations call to mind the jewels that were worn on the breastplate of the high priest to represent the 12 tribes of Israel. Eight stones in John's list are the same as those on the breastplate (Exodus 28:17).

There is also another interesting aspect of these stones. There was an ancient eastern myth about the city of the gods. Connected with it were the signs of the zodiac. The stones John saw in his heavenly vision are the same stones as those that correspond with the zodiac. Scholar William Barclay says there is "at least the possibility that John was thinking of the city of God as the consummation of the old idea of the city of the gods, but far outshining it."[5]

But there is an outstanding feature of John's listing of the precious stones. The order of the stones is reversed from those of the zodiac! God is saying to astrologers, "You've got the future figured out all wrong!" How futile indeed to chart your future by the stars. Chart your course by the direction of the Lord.

The Star of Bethlehem

An astronomical sign accompanied the birth of Jesus. The Magi from the East were drawn to Bethlehem by the appearance of a star. The Magi were Persian holy men and teachers of the kings. They were trained in philosophy, medicine and natural science.

When they arrived at Jerusalem they inquired, "Where is the one who has been born king of the Jews? We saw his star in the east and have come to worship him" (Matthew 2:2). Matthew stresses that God was at work in this astronomical sign. In fact, the Bible has a lot to say about the stars and how God reveals Himself in the heavens.

God made the stars (Genesis 1:16). The universe is 30 billion light years across. It consists of 100 billion galaxies, each containing hundreds of billions of stars. God calls each of the stars by name (Isaiah 40:26). Our galaxy, the Milky Way, has 400 stars, each with its own set of planets. The closest star is Alpha Centauri. The brightest star is Sirius, the Dog Star, which is nine light-years from earth. (In case you're interested, one light-year equals about 6 trillion miles!)

The star Epsilon is larger than the orbit of Pluto. If it were hollow it would contain 23 billion of the earth's suns! No wonder David proclaimed in praise, "The heavens declare the glory of God; the skies proclaim the work of his hands" (Psalm 19:1).

When I ponder the cosmos, I declare, "God is so great and I am so small!" Yet, God has numbered the hairs on my head and knows my thoughts before I think them. He is familiar with all my ways. Before I was born, He knew me even as I was being formed in my mother's womb. The God who inhabits the universe, who calls each star by name, knows each of us and lives in us when we put our trust in Him. What a miracle of miracles!

Astronomers have speculated on the mysterious star of Bethlehem that appeared around the time of the birth of Christ around 3 B.C. One theory is that the star was actually the conjunction of Jupiter and Saturn dated c. 7 B.C. Another explanation is based on the astronomical phenomenon that occurred between 5 and 2 B.C. On the first day of the Egyptian month Mesori, Sirius, the Dog Star, rose at sunrise and shone with an extraordinary brilliance. Interestingly, *Mesori* means, "birth of a prince." The ancients believed it was a sign from God announcing the birth of a king.

Whatever the case, an astronomical sign did appear and God used it to confirm the coming of the Messiah into the world. The Magi from the east certainly believed the star of Bethlehem was a sign that God was doing something special in the world. So, they traveled hundreds of miles to worship the Messiah in Bethlehem.

How did they know to go to Bethlehem? Were they guided by the zodiac? Absolutely not! They knew that the Messiah would be born in Bethlehem based on the prophecy of the Old Testament prophet, Micah, who ministered between 750 and 686 B.C.

> But you, Bethlehem Ephrathah, though you are small among the clans of Judah, out of you will come for me one who will be ruler over Israel, whose origins are from of old, from ancient times (Micah 5:2).

He predicted the exact location of Messiah's birth and revealed His divinity. His origins, or His "goings out," have been from ancient times, which can be translated from the Hebrew, "from days of eternity."

The Jews were carried into Babylonian captivity in 586 B.C. After 70 years of captivity, the Medes and Persians overthrew Babylon. Cyrus the Great, king of Persia, allowed the Jews to return home to Israel. The Persian government even paid for the rebuilding of the Temple and the wall of Jerusalem, as recorded in the Biblical books of Ezra and Nehemiah.

Many Jews remained in Babylon instead of going back to Israel. During the exile, Jewish rabbis and scribes taught the Scriptures and the hope of Messiah's coming. The understanding that Messiah would be born in Bethlehem was common knowledge. I'm quite certain that many Jewish rabbis and Persian Magi dialogued often about their beliefs. The Magi knew that Bethlehem was the selected place for the Messiah's birth because of the Scripture, not the stars. The Scripture led them; the star was only a divine confirmation. God leads our lives through the Scripture, not the stars.

The star also confirmed the prophecy of the Messiah given in Numbers 24:17, "A star will come out of Jacob; a scepter will rise out of Israel." Jesus reveals Himself in the Book of Revelation, by saying, "I am the Root and the Offspring of David, and the bright Morning Star" (22:16).

D. James Kennedy, in *The Real Meaning of the Zodiac,* gives an insightful depiction of the ministry of Christ in the signs of the zodiac. He says the word *zodiac* "comes from a primitive root, *zoad,* which comes from the Hebrew *sodi,* and in Sanskrit means: 'a way,' 'a path,' 'a step.' At a deeper level we see the zodiac picturing The Path, The Way of Salvation revealed beautifully for us in the heavens."[6]

While Aries is the starting point of the zodiac, Kennedy challenges this assumption. Since the zodiac is a circle, who can say where the beginning and ending points are? In the Temple of Esneh in Egypt, there is a sky painting in the portico on the ceiling bearing the signs of the zodiac. Between Virgo, the Virgin, and Leo, the Lion, there is carved the figure of the sphinx with the head of a woman and the body of a lion. The woman's face is looking at the virgin and the lion's tail is pointing at Leo, indicating that the zodiac begins with Virgo and ends with Leo.

Using this approach, Kennedy interprets the 12 ancient signs to tell the story of the gospel in the stars.

Virgo (the Virgin)—the seed of the Virgin. This sign depicts Jesus as the incarnate Son of God who was born of the Virgin Mary.

Libra (the Scales)—the price of redemption. This sign reveals Christ as the Redeemer who paid the full price for our sins.

Scorpio (the Scorpion)—the conquest over Satan at the Cross. Christ triumphed over Satan at the Cross to gain humanity's deliverance.

Sagittarius (the Archer)—the ultimate victory. This sign portrays Jesus as conqueror over sin and Satan on humanity's behalf.

Capricorn (the Goat-Fish)—life out of death. This sign reveals that through Christ's death and resurrection we have eternal life.

Aquarius (the Water-Pourer)—life and blessing out of Christ's victory. God has poured out His Spirit in our hearts as a mighty flowing river and dwells within us as a perpetual fountain of living water.

Pisces (the Fishes)—deliverance from captivity. This sign tells the story of God's deliverance of humanity from the bondage of sin through the preaching of the gospel of Christ.

Aries (the Lamb)—glory out of humiliation. Christ, the crucified lamb, has risen as the triumphant lion of the tribe of Judah and Lord of all creation.

Taurus (the Bull)—the glorious return of Christ. This sign foretells the second coming of Christ in power and glory as a raging bull in final judgment.

Gemini (the Twins)—fellowship with the church, Christ's bride. This sign represents the fellowship of Jesus with His people in eternity.

Cancer (the Crab)—the promise of the Kingdom. This sign assures us of God's promise that we will rule and reign with Him throughout eternity as a part of a multitude from every people, nation and language.

Leo (the Lion)—Christ's enemies destroyed. Prophetically, this sign promises that Christ, the lion of the tribe of Judah, will conquer every enemy, the last of which is death, and we will share eternity with Him.

Psychics and Cards

The reading of Tarot cards and the consulting of psychics is emerging along with astrology as a primary source for counseling and guidance. Cable networks and websites feature a host of readers and psychics who stand ready to assist inquirers in discovering their cosmic destinies.

The term *psychic* is used to describe mental phenomena that are or appear to be independent of normal sensory stimuli and include clairvoyance, telepathy and extrasensory perception (ESP). The term *PSI*, the 23rd letter of the Greek alphabet, is a general New Age term for ESP, psychokinesis, telepathy, clairvoyance, and other paranormal phenomena.

A psychic is one who claims such extraordinary powers and who can assist persons in knowing the future. Such mental powers are typically associated with the occult. The term *occult* refers to hidden or secretive wisdom and to that which is beyond the range of ordinary human knowledge acquired through the five senses. The occult includes such arts as psychic prediction, astrology, palmistry, spiritism, the I-Ching and so forth.

Three main features distinguish the occult. First, persons can experience revelation beyond the use of the five senses. Second, persons are placed in contact with supernatural powers, paranormal energies (such as spirit guides), or demonic forces. Third, power is mastered for the purpose of manipulating, controlling or influencing other people to act in certain ways.[7]

Occult practices seek to be legitimate by claiming to be scientific. The occult has sought refuge in the haven of parapsychology. However, the "very character of the occult indicates that it deals with contradictory or dissonant knowledge claims that are difficult, if not impossible, to investigate or validate."[8]

The occult worldview, which is predominant in Eastern philosophy and religion, is diametrically opposed to the worldview given in Scripture. Occult philosophy and its contemporary version found in New Ageism advocates a cosmic humanism. The occult worldview includes five major beliefs:

95

- The promise of godhood—man is a divine being.

- God is in everything (pantheism)—all is one.

- Life's purpose is to achieve awareness of the divine within, called self-realization, through illumination, enlightenment and oneness with the universe.

- Humanity is basically good—evil is an illusion.

- Self-realization, through spiritual techniques as meditation, chanting and yoga, leads to power, which is defined as the God-man being in charge.[9]

Tarot cards are another popular method of foretelling the future. Tarot cards are a deck of picture cards which was developed in its present form in the 20th century. The deck includes 22 characters, among them the Magician, Death, the Pope, the Popess, the Devil and the Fool. These can represent any person on the path of life.

Tarot is similar to the Chinese I-Ching, a book of divination. The ancient system of telling fortunes involved throwing sticks into six-sided figures. The I-Ching is based on Taoism. Tao, pronounced "dow," is the Chinese concept of the Way, which is both a path of conduct and the principle governing the entire universe.[10]

The Bible acknowledges the reality of occult practices. Pharaoh's magicians imitated the first of Moses' miracles. The witch of Endor conducted a séance for King Saul. But the Bible condemns these practices.

Moses issued a stern warning against those who would practice the ways of the occult.

When you enter the land the Lord your God is giving you, do not learn to imitate the detestable ways of the nations there. Let no one be found among you who . . . practices divination (fortune-telling) or sorcery, interprets omens, engages in witchcraft, or casts spells, or who is a medium (psychic or channeler) or spiritist or who consults the dead. . . . You must be blameless before the Lord your God (Deuteronomy 18:9-11, 13, parentheses added).

When we consider any such mystical powers, it is important to remember that Jesus Christ has "disarmed the powers and authorities . . . triumphing over them by the cross" (Colossians 2:15). When God gives a predictive message through the gift of prophecy, it always brings glory to Him. Astrology and psychic prediction bring no glory to God and serve only the interests of those who seek to control others through the occult.

Let me point out that God does make Himself known through divine revelation, which transcends the five senses. But God's revelations concern Himself and His will so that we might know Him more fully and that we might be conformed to the image of Christ. Paul prayed, that "the glorious Father, may give you the Spirit of wisdom and revelation, *so that you may know him better.* I pray also that the eyes of your heart may be enlightened in order that you may know the hope to which he has called you, the riches of his glorious inheritance in the saints, and his incomparably great power for us who believe" (Ephesians 1:17-19, emphasis added). Spiritual revelation is the work of the Holy Spirit, not the work of an astrologer or a psychic.

Walking by Faith, Not by Sight

Everyone is interested in the future. As believers, our task is not to know the future; it is to know what God is doing in the present. No psychic, astrologer or diviner can reveal your future or provide you the guidance you seek. The future does not belong to the stars but to the Maker of the stars. Your future cannot be predicted because it is not predetermined. Astrologers and psychics cannot predict anyone's future. They only manipulate persons into believing that their lives have some mystical, cosmic destiny.

Choice, not chance, nor the constellations, determines a person's future. You determine your future by the choices you make every day. In Christ, we are free from psychic prediction, from negative circumstances, from the mind control of others and from past experiences. God promises to guide us if we trust Him. He expects us to live by faith and not by sight (2 Corinthians 5:7). That includes what we see in the stars.

The Holy Spirit is our Counselor who guides us into all truth (John 16:13). We need only to look to God for wisdom in making decisions, and then to trust the direction He gives. Your life is *not* predetermined. Your life is being lived today, and only today. So walk by faith today, and God will lead you safely into tomorrow.

Near the end of World War II, King George VI delivered a radio address to the British Commonwealth on Christmas Eve. He challenged Britain's leaders to trust God.

> I said to the man who stood at the Gate of the Year, "Give me a light that I may tread safely into the unknown." And he replied, "Go out into the darkness, and put your hand

into the hand of God, and it shall be to you better than light, and safer than a known way."

At the time he spoke these words, his listeners knew he was dying of cancer. He had learned to walk by faith and not by sight. Put your hand in the hand of God and trust Him to order your steps in His will.

Look to the Savior, not to the stars!

Joseph Smith

6

When the Mormons Come Knocking

Everyone recognizes them. They're easy to spot. They travel in twos, are clean-cut with black suits and white shirts, and bear the title "elder." These Mormon missionaries zealously carry their message. Their sincerity is unquestionable, even envied by some. For two years, they devote themselves to spreading the message of Mormonism.

Mormonism is one of the world's richest and fastest growing religious movements. Last year alone, Mormon missionaries won more than 306,000 converts. Jeffrey Sheler notes that during its 170 year history, Mormonism has sustained the most rapid growth for a new faith group in American history with a worldwide membership of 11 million (half it's membership is outside the United States), 100 Mormon temples, over 12,000 local churches or meetinghouses throughout the world, and corporate assets estimated between $25 billion to $30 billion.[1]

Some people get involved in Mormonism, thinking innocently that it is simply another Christian denomination. Many are completely unaware of what Mormonism actually believes and advocates. How wide is the divide between mainstream Christianity and the teachings of Mormonism?

A significant book was written a few years ago to help both Christian's and Mormons understand each others' beliefs. The book, *How Wide the Divide? A Mormon and Evangelical in Conversation,* is an interaction between Stephen E. Robinson, a noted Mormon scholar for the Church of Jesus Christ of Latter-day Saints (LDS), and professor of ancient Scripture at Brigham Young University; and Craig L. Blomberg, a respected Christian scholar and a noted professor at Denver Seminary.

Blomberg sets forth clearly the historical and orthodox Christian view of such themes as the nature of God, the inspiration of Scripture, the person and ministry of Jesus Christ, salvation by grace through faith, and the Holy Trinity. But Robinson's contribution makes the waters murky on Mormon beliefs, unveiling the glaring errors and inconsistencies in Mormon theology.

While Mormon leaders argue that they are indeed a part of the Christian church, mainstream Christianity has rejected Mormonism as being outside the realm of orthodox Christianity. Recently, the 8.4 million-member United Methodist Church declared that Mormonism "by self-definition, does not fit within the bounds of the historical, apostolic traditions of the Christian faith."[2]

Jeffery L. Sheler, in the *U. S. News and World Report* article "The Mormon Moment," notes that "Mormon leaders readily concede that LDS doctrine differs substantially

102

from that of traditional Christianity which, they believe, went astray soon after the death of Jesus' apostles." According to Mormon spokesman Michael Otterson, their unique teaching "is an essential part of our message to the world that the Church of Jesus Christ has been restored in this latter-day period of the Earth's history."[3]

Mormons revere the teachings of Joseph Smith over those of Jesus as recorded by Matthew, Mark, Luke, John and the great apostles, Paul and Peter. According to Mormonism, Christians (called Gentiles) were misguided by an inadequate gospel and an inferior body of Scripture until Joseph Smith received his revelation from the angel Moroni and from Jesus' personal appearances to him. His position of, "I am right, and everyone else is wrong" is a common characteristic among cult leaders who claim to have received the only truth.

Let's begin at the beginning and take an honest look at the Mormon movement.

Meet Joseph Smith and Brigham Young

Joseph Smith Jr. is the founder of the Mormon movement. As a young boy of 15, in Manchester, New York, he claimed to have his first "heavenly visitation." It marked a series of numerous further revelations, which have since been incorporated in the foundation of Mormonism. He is called the first prophet, apostle and restorer.

Most of his revelations are recorded in the book *Doctrine and Covenants* (1830-1836), one of the several Mormon addenda to the Bible. Almost all the 136 sections begin with the words, "Revelation given to Joseph

Smith. . . ." His prophecies and teachings, however, are marked by serious theological error, fictional history and erroneous prophecies. As opposed to receiving divine revelation, Smith relied on published articles in both newspapers and magazines.

The prophecy in *Doctrine and Covenants,* Section 87, is marked by historical error in light of what really happened during the war. He also prophesied that he would possess the house he built in Nauvoo "forever and ever." The fact is, neither Smith nor his seed lived after him for "generation to generation" in the Nauvoo house, which was destroyed after Smith's death and the Mormons moved to Utah.[4]

In an effort to explain the contradictory statements and false prophecies made by Joseph Smith, a Mormon leader by the name of LeGrand Richards writes in *Marvelous Work and a Wonder,* "This glorious principle . . . did not come to the prophet Joseph Smith by reading the Bible, but through the revelation of the Lord." Richards claims that the revelations of Smith are superior to those of the Bible. This is the first tenet, which ultimately leads Mormonism away from solid Christian beliefs based on Scripture.[5]

Such contradictions between Smith's prophecies and the Bible include these erroneous Mormon doctrines:

- Eternal marriage (see Matthew 22:30)

- A human priesthood apart from the priesthood of Christ (see Hebrews 4:14)

- A selective male priesthood excluding women and African-Americans (which has been amended for African-Americans; see 1 Peter 2:9)

- The traditional teaching on polygamy (a practice officially abolished in 1890 but is still practiced by some in remote areas of the nation; see 1 Timothy 3:2),

- The keeping of endless genealogies (see v. 4)

- Proxy baptism on behalf of the dead as "a first step toward their ultimate acceptance into the faith," and others.

When the beliefs and practices of Mormonism, and Joseph Smith in particular, are weighed against the Scripture, they fail the test of truth.

Mormonism met strong rejection and opposition in its earlier years. In his revelations (which he claims were given to him by God the Father and by Jesus Christ), Joseph Smith vehemently attacked Christianity, boldly asserting that all churches and creeds were an "abomination" to the Lord.

He claimed to be a true prophet who had been ordained by God to restore the true gospel to the church (a common theme in every religious cult group). His opposition to the church put him in an adversarial role from the outset of his movement—an adversarial posture the Mormon church would like to remedy today. Mormon leaders court the favor of governments and social institutions in an effort to overcome the negative stigma of their past.

Mormonism seeks a mainstream position, boasting the largest private university in America, the Brigham

Young University. Mormons operate the largest religious media operation in the world, featuring the world-renowned Mormon Tabernacle Choir along with captivating television commercials advocating family values. The FBI and CIA recruit heavily among Mormons because of their sound morals.

Joseph Smith was murdered by an angry mob in Carthage, Illinois, in 1844. After Smith's untimely death, Brigham Young was elected to succeed Smith, until the church split. Young led his followers to Utah where he established the church. He encouraged polygamy, took 25 wives, and by the time he died in 1877, the movement had gained 140,000 adherents. Utah was denied statehood until the church officially abandoned its practice of polygamy in 1890.

The other group formed the Reorganized Church, claiming direct succession from Joseph Smith Jr. To date, nearly a hundred groups have splintered off from the original church.

What did Joseph Smith actually claim? In 1823, he claimed that the angel Moroni (not mentioned in Scripture) appeared at his bedside. The angel claimed to be the son of Mormon, a deceased leader of an American race known as Nephites. He also spoke to Smith about a book of golden plates containing "the fullness of the everlasting Gospel."

Four years later, near Palmyra, New York, Smith claimed he unearthed these plates, along with a supernatural pair of glasses, which he called the Urim and Thummim. (In Scripture, the Urim and Thummim were actually stones used by the High Priest of Israel in casting lots for decisions—see Exodus 28:29, 30.) Smith claimed he used the glasses to translate the hieroglyphics on the plates, a language he called "reformed Egyptian." (Archaeologists and Egyptologists deny that any such language ever existed.)

As he worked on the translation, he claimed that John the Baptist was sent by Peter, James and John to visit him and that John ordained him into the ministry. When the translation work was complete, with the assistance of Oliver Cowdery, an itinerant school teacher, and Erma Hale, his first and only legal wife, Smith claimed he returned the plates to the angel Moroni. *The Book of Mormon* was the result of the translation work which was published in 1830.

The subtitle, "Another Testament of Jesus Christ," was added recently to make *The Book of Mormon* appear to be more closely aligned with the Bible. On April 6, 1830, Oliver Cowdery, Joseph Smith, and his brothers Hyram and Samuel, officially formed the Church of Jesus Christ, now know as the Church of Jesus Christ of Latter-day Saints (LDS).[6]

The Book Of Mormon

The Book of Mormon is the cornerstone of Mormon faith and practice, along with other writings by Joseph Smith such as *Doctrines and Covenants* and *The Pearl of Great Price*. Tragically, *The Book of Mormon* is considered by its adherents to be superior to the Bible. When it contradicts the teachings of Scripture, *The Book of Mormon* is considered to be the final authority on matters of faith and life.

The Book of Mormon tells the story of two fabled mid-eastern groups who migrated to the Americas between 600 B.C. and A.D. 400. The Jaredites supposedly came from the Tower of Babel to Central America. They perished for their immorality.

A later group of Jews, led by a righteous man named Nephi, fled Jerusalem during the Babylonian captivity (586 B.C.) and ended up in South America. They divided into two warring factions, the Nephites and Lamanites. The Lamanites destroyed the Nephites in a fierce battle near Palmyra, New York, in A.D. 428. The victory earned them the curse of dark skin. They became the American Indians, according to the Mormon myth.

Before his demise, Mormon, the leader of the Nephites, recorded the history of his people and of the appearance of Jesus to them after His resurrection. According to Smith, this history was recorded on the golden plates he claimed to have discovered. However, no historical or archeological evidence exists to confirm this story, and it is regarded by historians as fiction.[7]

The contradictions between *The Book of Mormon* and *The Bible* are too numerous to enumerate in this chapter. A number of excellent works have undertaken the task very thoroughly. *The Book of Mormon* claims to be equal with the Bible as the "sealed book" referenced in Isaiah 29:11, and a record of the "other sheep" that Jesus said he had which were not a part of His original fold of followers (John 10:16).

The Book of Mormon is filled with verbatim quotes from the King James Version of the Bible (dated A.D. 1611), although Smith claimed it had been written many centuries before. The analogous passages include some 17th century translators' errors, clearly revealing that *The Book of Mormon* was written after the date claimed for its origin.

The Book of Mormon also asserts that these immigrants produced metal, a claim not supported by archaeology. It even describes elephants roaming the Western Hemisphere, though no skeletons have ever been found. The Smithsonian Institute unequivocally denies the historical claims made in *The Book of Mormon*. *The Book of Mormon* is clearly a fictitious story, which merges fiction and portions of Scripture with the radical religious views of Joseph Smith.

So who wrote *The Book of Mormon,* and where did Joseph Smith get his fictional history? Some scholars believe that Smith borrowed material from the King James Bible and 19th-century historical speculation to produce a novel. Most students of Mormonism, however, believe that the *Book of Mormon* is "probably an expansion upon the writings of Solomon Spaulding, a retired minister who was known to have written a number of 'romances' with Biblical backgrounds similar to those written in the *Book of Mormon.*" This is the predominant view of evangelical critics who note that Smith always dictated his writings from behind a curtain, enabling him to conceal the actual source of his dictation.[8]

Finally, scholars point out that Smith's writings bear a marked similarity to those of the Reverend Ethan Smith, author of *View of the Hebrews.* Some critics make the case that Joseph Smith, a former Mason, drew heavily on Masonic rituals rather than divine revelation when he instituted Mormon temple rites. These rites do, in fact, bear strong resemblance to many Masonic rituals.[9]

Who Is God?

The God of Mormonism is far removed from the God of
the Bible. Mormonism teaches that God is a physical, material being. He is a procreating father with a divine mother-
wife. Humans are believed to be preexistent spirits begotten
by God. This belief explains the strong Mormon emphasis
on marriage and parenthood in this life and the next.

According to Joseph Smith, God "is an exalted man"
who "was once as we are now."[10] Lorenzo Snow, a successor of Joseph Smith, states, "As man now is, God once
was; as God now is, man may become."[11] Such statements represent the height of false doctrine, making God
and man the same.

Brigham Young taught that Adam was actually God
who assumed a body and came to the Garden of Eden
(which he locates in Missouri) with Eve, one of his heavenly wives. It was this same Adam-God (who he also
identifies as Michael, the archangel) who conceived
Jesus through sexual relations with the Virgin Mary. "He
[Christ] was not begotten by the Holy Ghost," Young
emphatically stated.[12]

Mormonism denies the transcendence of God over
His creation. What is more, Mormonism seeks to make
the Creator one with the creation. The apostle Paul con-
fronts such error:

> For although they knew God, they neither glorified him
> as God nor gave thanks to him, but their thinking became
> futile and their foolish hearts were darkened. Although
> they claimed to be wise, they became fools and exchanged
> the glory of the *immortal God* for images *made to look
> like mortal man*" (Romans 1:21-23, emphasis added).

110

But God and man are not and will never be the same. True, humanity is created in the image of God, not by some mythical procreation, but through the spoken word of God (Hebrews 11:3). God formed man in His own image out of the dust of the ground. God is eternal; man is temporal. God is spirit; man is flesh. God is not material, nor does He procreate as man does. Jesus clearly taught that "God is spirit, and his worshipers must worship in spirit and in truth" (John 4:24).

Further, Mormonism asserts that humans can become gods in the next life through baptism, good works and eternal marriage; and can create and sustain their own universe through procreation. This is pure polytheism, the belief in many gods as opposed to the Biblical revelation of the one true God. Strangely, Mormons even believe that Jesus was married to both Martha and Mary and that He had children. Mormons enter marriage using Masonic-like rituals, which seal their marriages for eternity.[13]

The beliefs of polytheism and polygamy go hand in hand in early Mormon teaching. Brigham Young claimed: "The only men who become gods are those who enter into polygamy." Today, Utah is pocketed with an estimated 30,000 fundamentalist Mormons who still practice polygamy. They believe they will be kept out of heaven unless they observe the covenant of polygamy prescribed by Joseph Smith.[14]

Mormon doctrine on the nature of God contradicts the high and holy view of Scripture of the one true God: "Now to the King eternal, immortal, invisible, the only God be, honor and glory for ever and ever. Amen" (1 Timothy 1:17).

Some modern Mormon theologians appear to contradict Joseph Smith and Brigham Young on the subject of the nature of God. For example, Mormon theologian, Stephen E. Robinson, in *How Wide the Divide? A Mormon and an Evangelical in Conversation*, says that in addition to God being physical, "God is omniscient, omnipotent, omnipresent, infinite and eternal and unchangeable."

But how can God be both physical and omnipresent? That's impossible. Physicality means, inherently, to be limited by time, space and matter. But Robinson does contradict Joseph Smith who stated in *The King Follett Discourse*, that God by nature is changeable, finite, contingent, not eternally God, and corporeal and that humans too can become gods.[15]

The Mormon doctrine of polytheism clearly places it outside the boundaries of orthodox Christianity. The fall of Adam by eating the forbidden fruit was what made him capable of fathering the human race. According to Mormons, "God himself was once procreated in another world, and now humans may aspire to the status of procreator that he has obtained . . . in other words, 'Adam fell that men might be.' The right to godhead is not earned by the grace of Jesus but by being a good Mormon" which means "being baptized and married in temple, being a member of the priesthood, and tracing genealogies." As potential father and mother gods, Mormons believe they will one day have their own planets to populate.[16]

The most fundamental fact of faith in the Bible is that God is one: "The Lord our God, the Lord is one" (Deuteronomy 6:4). By teaching that men can become gods in the next life, and join a pantheon of gods, Mormonism distinguishes itself as a polytheistic religion. Christianity and Judaism are monotheistic religions. We believe there is one God, eternally revealed in three Persons—Father, Son and Holy Spirit—who alone is Creator, Redeemer and Father.

Mormons need to heed the God of the Bible when He confronted the polytheistic pagan religions which threatened Israel's faith during the time of Isaiah the prophet: "Before me no god was formed, nor will there be one after me. I, even I, am the Lord, and apart from me there is no savior" (Isaiah 43:10, 11). And Isaiah reassured the people saying, "Surely God is with you, and there is no other; there is no other god" (45:14).

But some will say, doesn't the Bible call men gods? Yes, Psalm 82:6 says, "I said, 'You are 'gods'; you are all sons of the Most High." Who are these "gods?" Scholars have suggested three possibilities: the false gods of paganism, the fallen angels who rebelled with Lucifer, or unjust and wicked rulers who oppressed the poor and weak. The Canannites of Old Testament times considered the gods to be sons of the Most High. But this psalm makes it clear that they cannot be sons of God because they do not reflect the concerns of God with justice, morality and order.[17]

Jesus taught that this psalm refers to unjust human rulers (see John 10:34). They were only "gods," in the sense that they were "mighty ones." The same word is used to describe angels as "mighty ones" (Psalm 29:1). This does not mean that men or angels are divine, or that they can attain divinity. In fact, listen to the next statement God makes to these unjust leaders called *gods*, "But you will

die like mere men; you will fall like every other ruler"
(82:7). In their arrogance, they saw themselves as gods,
but they would perish like all men.

Men will never become gods in eternity. Such a notion
has more in common with Greek mythology than with
the Bible, and must be denounced as the height of unbiblical doctrine.

We would do well at this point to reflect on Paul's
words concerning the greatness of the one true and living
God: "There is but one God, the Father, from whom all
things came and for whom we live; and there is but one
Lord, Jesus Christ, through whom all things came and
through whom we live" (1 Corinthians 8:6). The three
erroneous doctrines of polytheism, polygamy and procreation set Mormonism on the wrong track theologically
from its very beginning. Here's the "fly in the ointment"
with Mormon beliefs. Stephen Robinson says:

> The official word or authority on matters of theology
> resides with the 'living prophet' [that is, the current pres-
> ident of the Mormon church], and only secondarily in the
> preservation of the written text. What God has said to
> apostles and prophets in the past is always secondary to
> what God is saying to his apostles and prophets now."[18]

Mormon theology, then, is always subject to change by
a new pronouncement by the living prophet (the LDS
president). Such theology is evolutionary in nature and
subject to change, unlike the changeless truth of Scripture.
Paul declared, "All Scripture is God-breathed and is useful
for teaching, rebuking, correcting and training in righteousness, so that the man of God may be thoroughly equipped
for every good work" (2 Timothy 3:16, 17).

Life After Death

Mormon teaching on the afterlife is one of the most attractive features of the movement today. Mormons are universalists who believe that every person will eventually have eternal life, but only baptized Mormons will become gods. The LDS article of faith, number three states, "We believe that through the Atonement of Christ, all mankind may be saved."

The only exception is the "sons of perdition." Mormons who depart from the faith will suffer eternal punishment. Everyone else will at least enter the "telestial kingdom," which, in the words of Jeffery Sheler, is "a sort of a third-rate paradise where one spends eternity apart from God." The most faithful will inherit the "celestial kingdom," where they "commune directly with God and may themselves become gods and inherit universes to rule and populate with their own spiritual offspring."

They believe that families can be bound together "for time and eternity" if they undergo a special "sealing" ritual in the Mormon temple. In this world, their families are expected to conduct weekly "family home evenings" for parents and children to play, pray and study Scripture or the *Book of Mormon*. Their family emphasis, and the idea that families can be together throughout eternity, is attractive and comforting to many people.[19]

According to Mormon teaching, every person will receive a second chance in the afterlife to believe the gospel and to receive eternal rewards. This is why Mormons practice baptism for the dead in proxy on behalf of their ancestors who died as unbelievers. This would include all who lived before the full revelation of truth was given to Joseph Smith.

Mormons also go to great lengths to research their genealogies so that they can be baptized in proxy for their deceased ancestors. The church maintains its largest physical facility in Salt Lake City, Utah. It is devoted exclusively to housing the ancestral records of devout Mormons. It has hundreds of millions of microfilmed records used by its many members to identify their non-Mormon ancestors for proxy baptism.

Yet, their beliefs regarding the afterlife contradict the truth of Scripture. As painful as it is to grasp, everyone will not inherit eternal life. Jesus gave the most graphic description of eternity with God in his account of the rich man and Lazarus (Luke 16:19-31). The Book of Revelation clearly teaches the reality of both heaven and hell (see 19:11–21:7).

Furthermore, the only reference to baptism for the dead is found in Paul's corrective teachings to the misguided believers at Corinth, who apparently had mistakenly incorporated a pagan ritual into the church (see 1 Corinthians 15:29). The early church did not practice the rite of baptism for the dead.

Finally, Mormons believe in three levels of heaven. The first level is for the pagans; the second, for non-Mormon Christians; and the third is reserved for faithful, baptized Mormons with sealed eternal marriages who will create and rule universes. But nowhere in Scripture do we read of different levels of heaven—celestial or telestial—as presented in Mormon doctrine.

The apostle Paul does speak of the "third heaven" in his writings (see 2 Corinthians 12:2). This is not to be confused with the Mormon view of heaven. Paul uses the term consistent with Hebrew theology. The three heavens consist of: The first heaven, the earth's atmosphere; the second heaven, the realm of angels and demons; and the third heaven, the eternal dwelling of God. All true believers are promised entrance into the kingdom of heaven—not on the basis of their works, baptism or ritualism, but by the grace of God through faith in Jesus Christ (see Romans 10:9-13; Ephesians 2:8-10).

Who Is Jesus?

The greatest doctrinal error of Mormonism is the distortion of the person and ministry of Jesus Christ. Jesus is the touchstone of truth. All religions and philosophies must be measured against him.

Paul cautions us about those who would preach "a Jesus other than the Jesus [the apostles] preached" (2 Corinthains 11:4). Clearly, Mormonism preaches a "different Jesus" than the Jesus of Scripture. They claim Jesus is a human creation of God and a brother of Lucifer. Joseph Smith wrote: "Among the children of Elohim, the firstborn was and is Jehovah or Jesus Christ, to whom all others are juniors."[20]

But Jehovah and Elohim are not two separate deities in the Old Testament, but rather simply different Hebrew names for God. The Hebrew names of God used in the Old Testament portray the wonders of His nature and power. Mormon error suggests that Elohim is the greater God, and Jehovah, or Jesus Christ, is the lesser God, who is the offspring of Elohim. Such an error reflects Smith's ignorance of the Hebrew language and the Old Testament usage of the names of God. In fact, the names Jehovah and Elohim are often compounded in the Old Testament as "the Lord God" (Jehovah—Lord; Elohim—God).[21]

Mormonism not only denies that Jesus is the second person of the Trinity, but also denies the Virgin Birth of our Savior. As stated earlier, Jesus is believed to be a spirit brother of Lucifer (as alluded to in *The Pearl of Great Price,* Moses 4:1-4, and reaffirmed by Brigham Young in the *Journal of Discourses,* Vol. 13, p. 282). Jesus is also believed to have been married to "the Marys and Martha, whereby he could see his seed before he was crucified."[22]

Some Mormon scholars articulate what appears to be, on the surface, a more orthodox view of Jesus. Mormon spokesman Michael Otterson says, "We revere Jesus Christ as the Son of God, the Redeemer and Savior of the world."[23] However, Mormon theology denies Jesus' unique sonship as the second member of the Holy Trinity, who is fully God and fully man. They use the same vocabulary, but with a different meaning.

Mormonism also falls short on its view of the sufficiency of Christ's atoning death for all the sins of the world. Brigham Young strongly believed in the highly controversial and now suppressed Mormon doctrine of "blood atonement." He believed Christ's blood could not atone for certain sins—sins that could only be atoned for by shedding man's blood.

Mormon scholars have since tried to explain and justify Young's view of blood atonement to make it more compatible with the Biblical teaching of the sufficiency of the blood of Christ to take away *all* sin. John the apostle assures us that "the blood of Jesus, his Son, purifies us from all sin" (1 John 1:7).

Mormons and the Bible

Mormon theology is rife with unbiblical beliefs, prophecies and statements made by Mormon leaders on a variety of subjects from Joseph Smith until now. Since Mormon theology is ever-evolving with new revelations by the current president of the church, called "the living prophet," such contradictions and inconsistencies are bound to exist between Mormon writings and the Bible.

Mormons claim to believe the Bible is the Word of God, but add that it must be interpreted correctly—that is, interpreted in light of Mormon theology. Joseph Smith attacked the Bible and orthodox Christianity as being erroneous, claiming that he had been ordained of God to restore the true gospel to a misguided church.

Mormons elevate the teachings of the *Book of Mormon* and other Mormon writings over the Bible. They lack a central source of inspired spiritual authority for their beliefs since they deny the inspiration, inerrancy and authority of Scripture.

The Restored Priesthood

Mormons believe in the restored priesthoods of the Biblical personalities of Aaron and Melchizedek. All Mormon males, 12 years or older, are eligible for the Aaronic priesthood. Those 18 years or older can enter the higher order of Melchizedek (a godly priest who was a contemporary of Abraham; see Genesis 14).

Until 1978, those with dark skin were forbidden this office. Joseph Smith taught that those with black skin were descendants of Cain and therefore cursed. Even the

Mormon temples were off limits to blacks until the change in their official position.[24]

The Book of Hebrews is clear that the priesthoods of both Melchizedek and Aaron are fulfilled in Jesus Christ, our great High Priest.[25] In addition, all believers are priests of God who are called to pray for others and minister the grace of God in Jesus' name. The Reformers called it, "the priesthood of all believers." It includes all Christians regardless of race, gender or age, not just a select few. "But you are a chosen people, a royal priesthood, a holy nation, a people belonging to God" (1 Peter 2:9). Jesus has made "us to be a kingdom and priests to serve his God and Father" (Revelation 1:6).

Current Trends

Mormons leaders are trying to improve their image. They seek to downplay the more radical and dark elements of their history and theology—such as polygamy, blood atonement and radical statements about Jesus being the brother of Lucifer—in an effort to present itself as mainstream Christianity.

Jeffery Sheler reports, "In 1995, leaders hired an international public relations firm to combat what they saw as unfair characterizations of Mormons in the media. One of its first efforts was to encourage the redesign of the church's logo to emphasize the centrality of Jesus Christ in LDS theology."[26]

But changing the image is quite different from changing the substance of the church's beliefs and practices. Such substantive changes will be the test of genuine reform. The real problem is, while Mormons use the same vocabulary as Christians, they often mean something radically different by the terms.

On a more positive note, some Mormon scholars advocate a critical reexamination of the church's history and origins. However, tighter controls by the church's headquarters limits the ability for such honest spiritual searching among their theologians, ministers and members. The church is highly intolerant toward those who raise objections. Professors at Brigham Young University have been dismissed for raising such objections.

Members who publicly question the church's teachings or criticize church leaders risk excommunication. Such intolerance has a "chilling effect on academic inquiry" within the church, says Elbert Peck, former editor of *Sunstone,* an independent Mormon journal.[27] I have personally witnessed the extreme intimidation that comes along with Mormon excommunication, and have counseled several persons who left the LDS church.

Mormonism is attractive to some people because of its emphasis on strong families and moral ethics, such as its opposition to smoking, alcohol, premarital sex and so forth. But this moral outer shell masks the core of their unorthodox beliefs. Unfortunately, many people today will sacrifice doctrinal accuracy for a religion that works. In reality, true Christianity offers both.

The winds of reform may be beginning to blow within the ranks of Mormonism, which could result in true reformation. Reformation means recanting all false teachings and accepting the true teachings of Christ found in Scripture. The current efforts by leaders to take the church mainstream may just be an open door for such true reforms. Some Mormons may leave the LDS church in their quest for a true relationship with God through the salvation of Jesus Christ. Many already have.

That brings us to the most important question of all, How are we to share our faith with Mormons?

Sharing Your Faith

Karl Alsin, in "When Cults Come Knocking," provides some excellent insights into witnessing to Mormons.[28] A former Mormon who became a Christian, his strategy is quite helpful as he draws on the experience of Jesus with the woman at the well (see John 4).

First, he believes that our goal is not necessarily to convert every Mormon who comes knocking on our doors. We may only have the opportunity to plant the seed of the gospel, while someone else may have the joy of leading them to Christ. So, relax. Share your faith without any pressure and let the Holy Spirit do the work. Your task is to plant the seed.

Start with the Scriptures. Karl suggests a simple method: *Have cult members read out loud from their Bible while you ask the questions.* We cannot make them accept the truth, but we can lead them to the truth.

Karl tells how his brother led him out of Mormonism while he was attending Brigham Young University. His brother simply asked him to read out loud a passage in Isaiah 44:6-8, which speaks of the one true God. His brother then asked Karl, "How many gods does God know about? If God knows of one God, how can the Mormons claim there are many gods?" The more Karl read the Bible, the more inconsistencies he found between Mormonism and the Bible. The Word did the work!

Karl also suggests that we take the initiative when cult members come knocking. "After they've introduced themselves, I tell them I have some questions I would like to discuss and ask them if they'd be willing to read something from their own Bibles. . . . Then I like to share briefly my testimony as a Christian and thank them for their time. I always ask them to return, which demonstrates sincerity and a desire to continue our discussion."

Take charge of the discussion. Ask them questions about the Bible. Use the material I have provided in this book to know the doctrines of cults and other religions. Show them love and concern. Be interested in their views and show them respect. They are genuinely seeking to know God and to find eternal life.

You will typically get memorized responses from persons involved in cults. Most have not critically examined their beliefs in light of the Bible. Stick to what you know. Don't get sidetracked by trying to answer questions about their religion. Tell them you don't know everything about their religious beliefs. Then direct them back to the Bible.

Remember: Everyone wants the assurance of eternal life. They don't have it. That's why they work to earn their salvation. But you have the assurance of eternal life. So, share that assurance with them. Focus on Jesus. They need to hear about Him. "Let your conversation be always full of grace, seasoned with salt, so that you may know how to answer everyone" (Colossians 4:6).

From Mormon to Disciple

After speaking one evening on the subject of Mormonism, a young man introduced himself to me and shared his story of how he came out of Mormonism into Christianity. I was so intrigued with his experience that I asked him to send me his whole story. He also granted me permission to share his testimony in this chapter in the hope that others may come to Christ. If you are witnessing to family or friends in Mormonism, I think you will find this young man's testimony a useful resource. His name is Brian.

I was born in Salt Lake City, Utah, to parents who are Polygamist Mormons. My father had four wives and 31 children. I was the 27th of the 31 children. My mother was my father's third wife. She had seven children, of which I was the youngest. They belong to a group of polygamists who separated from the LDS church after the church renounced polygamy. The first Mormon in my family line became a Mormon during Joseph Smith's lifetime. They came across the plains with the Mormon pioneers and helped settle much of Utah and Idaho.

As I grew up in this strange family, I found that there was great rivalry between the wives and their children. My mother and her children were at the bottom of the pecking order.

My father was a control freak and an abusive man. He ruled his house with fear. I remember how deathly afraid I was whenever he came home from work. I remember seeing the same fear in the eyes of my siblings. I was

blessed to be one of the youngest. And by the time I
came on the scene, my father had long since stopped caring about disciplining his children and reserved it for the
most drastic of cases. He seemed to take refuge in watching television.

My mother plotted her escape for many years. I was 13
when she asked me to leave with her. Without any need for
thought, my immediate answer was, "Yes, Mom, I'll go
with you. Anything is better than the hell I'm living in."

I never asked her why she was leaving. I was just glad to
be going. We moved in with my grandmother who had a
very large house that had been divided up into apartments.

I wanted to be there for my mother and sister, but I had
no idea how to help them. I figured I just had to be there
for them whenever they needed a shoulder.

I began drinking and taking drugs in an attempt to numb
out enough to be able to have a good time and not dwell
on my problems. At the age of 19, I joined the Navy to
get away from my family. I just wanted to get as far away
from them and my childhood as I could. I was stationed
in San Diego for four years. During my years in the
Navy, I was drinking very heavily and taking drugs. My
life was going downhill very fast.

After I got out of the Navy, I went home again. I went
from job to job, getting hired and laid off from construc-
tion jobs. At this point I became convinced that religion

was only a mind game used by other men to control people. I began to deny that God existed. I would shake my fist at God and shout out at the sky, saying, "God, you don't exist. God, if you do exist, I curse you!"

I later joined the Marine Corps and was once again getting away from my family. My sister, who had become a Christian, and I were talking together the night before I went off to boot camp. I was sitting in the front seat of her car crying like a baby, angry at life and at God. She listened as I poured out my broken heart. Then she said, "Brian, I know this doesn't make any sense to you right now. But one day you will come to know Jesus Christ as your Lord and Savior. And when you do, He will heal all the hurt you're feeling. He will remove it from you as far as the east is from the west. He will be to you the father you never had."

She told me the reason she knew Jesus could heal my broken heart was because He had healed hers. She was free to forgive my father for the abuse she suffered. Well, she was right. I wasn't able to understand.

I realized that I was blaming God for the evil things men had done. I had been judging God; something I had no place doing. I began looking into the Scriptures. I began to feel a need for God in my life. So, I joined the LDS Church while I was in boot camp, mainly because it was familiar to what I was used to.

My first year after boot camp was spent in Okinawa, Japan. I attended services there on and off again. I became aware that I could never say with full confidence that the LDS church was the true church. There were too many doubts because of the history of the LDS church that I knew far too well. I realized I was fooling myself into trying to believe in something I knew was wrong.

I knew there was a God out there somewhere who loved me and all I had to do was find Him. I stopped going to the LDS services because they were as empty as the ones I knew from childhood. All I knew was that the Spirit of God wasn't there. The spirit I felt there wasn't a spirit of love, but one of judgment or condemnation.

My next duty station was at Cherry Point, North Carolina. While I was stationed there I meet Dana, who later became my wife. When the news came that we were going to have an addition to our new family, the topic of religion came up. Dana and I both agreed that we had to be united in what we would teach our kids about God. But she was raised in a Christian home and I . . . well you know. She asked me what Mormons believe because she didn't know much about them. I got about as far as explaining the Mormon path to godhood when she said that she had heard enough and needed time to let it all sink in.

The next day she announced that she would never become a Mormon. To tell the truth I was relieved. I was afraid she would want to become a Mormon and I would be faced with going back to something I didn't believe in. I knew I didn't believe in Mormonism, but I also didn't know what to believe.

I only knew I believed there was a God, and that Jesus was his Son. Dana and I let religion slip to a back burner with the birth of our son, Sterling. With a long deployment coming up, we wanted to spend time together as a family before I had to go.

On deployment in the Texas desert, I learned that two of my fellow sergeants were Christians. They were reading a book by Hal Lindsey called, *The Late Great Planet Earth*. I had always been interested in end-time prophecy. I asked to borrow the book they were reading. As I read, I would discuss with them the different things I had learned from the book.

In the book, Hal does a great job of showing God's love for us, that God had provided a way for us to escape His wrath. If we believed in Jesus' atonement on the cross, we wouldn't suffer these things. While I was still a sinner, Jesus died to reconcile me to God. While I was cursing Him, He still loved me. I was so overcome by the love of God that I wept. But I still had a lot to work through before I would accept the free gift God was offering me. After I returned, I told Dana about the book I'd read and the way God had touched my heart.

Dana and Sterling were able to join me and as soon as we got settled into our home, we both felt the need to find a church we could agree on attending. I told her that the only thing I knew to believe was that there was a God and that His Son, Jesus Christ, died for my sins on the cross. As long as they are teaching the Bible and that Jesus was the Son of God, then I didn't have a problem.

We searched but couldn't find a church both of us liked. Then one day Dana suggested a church that was about a half an hour away from us. Somehow, she convinced me to try it out. After the first service Dana was sure this was where God wanted us. On the second Sunday, Dana asked if we could join. I wasn't sure yet. The third Sunday, Dana got up and said that she was going to join with or without me because she knew God had led us to this church. So, we joined the church that day.

We started getting more involved in the church's Bible studies. I was learning more and more about a side of God I had never seen before. All my life I had seen God as a God of judgment and wrath. But now I was seeing God's love.

One day, Dana suggested that we attend a class about other religions. The winning argument was when she said that if I really wanted to understand the differences between Christians and Mormons, this class would be the perfect place. So, I went to the class. It happened to be the last day of the class and so they were reviewing what they had learned about other religions. I got as much literature as I could from the class because I was offended when I saw that they had labeled Mormonism as a cult.

I was going to look up all the references they gave and search the Scriptures to prove them wrong about the things they were saying about Mormonism. It wasn't because I still believed in Mormonism; it was because it was my whole identity. I felt that it was my duty to defend my family history. But the more I searched the Scriptures to prove them wrong, the more I proved them right.

I had come to a crossroads. I had to decide once and for all what I was—a Mormon or a Christian? I thought about this and wondered how to come to a decision. I finally decided that the only fair approach would be to study the two religions without any outside help. I looked up Scripture references and studied doctrinal views, and I found so many contradictions within Mormonism that it was clear to me it was a faith built on false doctrines. If the current prophet wanted to change something about the LDS church's doctrines, there wasn't anything he couldn't change.

But in Christianity, I saw a God who never changes, who is the same today as He was yesterday. I saw a God who loved me and was personal and real. It was through studying the differences between these two faiths that I found the love of God for me.

I decided I was going to become a Christian. But I didn't know how to become one. I had done independent studies on Islam, Buddhism, Catholicism, Jehovah's Witnesses, Hinduism and Mormonism. I had the intellectual knowledge that would lead me to salvation, but I had never made the connection that there was a heart application.

What mattered to God was my relationship with Him, and at this point in my life it wasn't a right relationship. But now that God had removed the scales from my eyes, I was prepared to meet Him on my Damascus-road experience.

One day I was praying on my way to work. It took me about 35 to 40 minutes to get there, and this was the time I had set aside to talk to God. I wanted to be free. And that was when God spoke to me through the Holy Spirit and asked me, "Brian, what's wrong?"

I said, "My life is a mess and You said You would make a new creation out of me. But I see no evidence of this in my life."

God asked me, "Brian, who paid for your sins?"

I said, "You did, Lord."

He said, "Did I not say I would make a new creation out of those who come to Me?"

I said, "Yes, Lord."

Then He said, "You already know that I paid for your sins. What's missing Brian? What haven't you done?"

I responded, "I've never confessed that you are my Lord. I've never asked You to come into my heart. I have never surrendered my life to You."

Then He said, "And you wonder why I can't change you and make you a new creature, why sin still rules your life? I can't fix what you haven't given me Brian!"

I said, "You mean that just because I haven't said that prayer, the sinner's prayer, You can't fix my life?"

Once again God said, "I can't fix what you haven't given me Brian!"

131

It was 5 a.m. and it was raining that morning—one of the hard downpours Okinawa is known for. I could barely see the road. My tears didn't make matters any better. So, I dried my eyes as I pulled off the road and surrendered my fight against God. I gave my life to Him and asked Him to change me from the inside out. And for the first time in my life, I realized that religion couldn't save me. Only a relationship with God could save me. And that relationship had to begin with the heart application of a total surrender of self to the Lordship of Jesus Christ.

I have been a Christian for five years now. And God has changed my life so radically that everyone I know says I'm not the same man they knew. God even gave me a heart that could love my father and forgive him. Today I look back at my life and see the road I've traveled, and I'm amazed at the mighty God I serve.

On Thanksgiving Day, I stood in the living room of my wife's grandparent's house. They were thanking God for what He has done. I told them what God had done in my life. For the first time I realized that the words my sister Mary spoke to me that night in her car before I went off to boot camp were words of prophecy.

She had said, "Brian, I know this doesn't make any sense to you right now. But one day you will come to know Jesus Christ as your Lord and Savior. And when you do, He will heal all the hurt you are feeling. He will remove it from you as far as the east is from the west. He will be to you the father you never had."

7

Who Are the Jehovah's Witnesses?

Charles T. Russell

When she was a small child my wife, Barbie, became critically ill. She was rushed to the hospital. Without a blood transfusion, she would die. But her aunt, then a staunch Jehovah's Witness, tried to prevent the blood transfusion based on her religious beliefs. (Jehovah's Witnesses consider blood transfusion the same as eating blood, which is forbidden in Leviticus 17:10-15.)

Fortunately, her father intervened, overcame the madness, and approved the transfusion. He actually gave his own blood to save his daughter's life. Years later, her aunt became a Christian and left the Jehovah's Witness movement.

Such a story makes you stop and ask, why are people misled by cults? Several reasons come to mind. First, people lack a solid faith based on Scripture, so they are easily deceived by the fine-sounding arguments presented by cults. Others lack spiritual discernment. They fail to ask critical questions or investigate the so-called "deep secrets" of cultic beliefs.

Most often people are lonely, looking for friends, or just want to belong to an important group or movement. This need to belong often leads people into such cults. Once a part of the group, members feel accepted and significant. They pledge their loyalty even though it means abdicating their personal freedom to the organization's hierarchy. Emotional needs often influence people's religious affiliations as much, if not more, than spiritual or intellectual needs.

Cults are born out of a discontented, deceived or disillusioned heart. Cult leaders invariably claim that they possess a new, divine revelation of truth. This means that everyone else is misguided and needs the leader's new revelation, without which they cannot be saved. Such is the case with the Jehovah's Witness movement.

Where It All Began

Charles Taze Russell began the Jehovah's Witnesses in 1879. The son of a clothing merchandiser in Pennsylvania, he had no formal theological training and only a 7th grade education. In his early '20s, he was influenced by the teachings of William Miller and the Adventist movement. Miller claimed that the second coming of Christ had occurred in 1843, but later changed the date to 1844. When it was obvious that Christ had not returned, the Adventists returned to Scripture and developed a new method of date setting by which to predict the Second Coming.

Among these Adventists was N.H. Barbour, with whom Russell collaborated to write *Three Worlds and the Harvest of This World* (1877). They claimed that Christ had returned "invisibly" in 1874 and that the golden age (the Millennium) could be expected in 1914. Christ rules the earth through the Witness movement headquartered in Brooklyn, New York. Russell held the position of president of the Jehovah's Witnesses for the rest of his life.

Russell parted company with orthodox Christian views of hell, the Holy Trinity and the deity of Jesus Christ. He began publishing his radical views in *The Herald of the Morning* magazine. By 1884 he controlled the magazine and renamed it *The Watchtower Among Jehovah's Kingdom.* He officially organized his group as "The Watch Tower Bible and Tract Society" that same year. As the first president of the Watchtower Society, he authored six volumes of the seven volume series, *The Studies in the Scriptures.* He claimed people would "go into darkness" if they studied the Bible without the aid of *The Studies.*[1]

How did Russell arrive at the original 1874 date for the Second Coming? He considered the Great Pyramid of Egypt to be prophetic in nature. He calculated the length of its corridors with historical events to arrive at the 1874 date, which also marked the beginning of the Great Tribulation, he said.

After Russell's death in 1916, the group abandoned the 1874 date for a later 1914 date. In a new edition of *The Studies* (1923), they simply recalculated the dimensions of the Great Pyramid, adding 41 inches to the corridor and reassessing the starting point of the earth's final years of existence to be 1914. Russell also claimed that the

144,000 would be sealed in 1914 as "kings and priests in heaven," and that those saved after 1914 would constitute a servant class under the rule of the 144,000.[2]

Obviously, Charles Russell was as wrong as wrong can be in regard to prophecy, and was a false prophet by Biblical standards. "If what a prophet proclaims in the name of the Lord does not take place or come true, that is a message the Lord has not spoken. That prophet has spoken presumptuously. Do not be afraid of him" (Deuteronomy 18:22).

The theology of Charles Russell forms much of the theological foundations of the Jehovah's Witnesses, who were originally called "Russellites." Today, however, the Jehovah's Witnesses dispute many of his teachings and distance themselves from their roots. Confusion exists over the influence of Charles Russell in the movement.

Walter Martin, in *Kingdom of the Cults,* notes: "Rutherford plainly quotes Russell and his writings as authoritative material, yet *The Watchtower* today claims that Jehovah's Witnesses are free from the taint of Russellism!"[3] Charles Russell, the founder and first president, once revered by the Jehovah's Witnesses, is now repudiated.

Joseph Franklin Rutherford, a Missouri lawyer, succeeded Russell as the next president of the movement. Like Russell, "Judge" Rutherford reached the point of unquestioned authority in his teachings. At a convention in 1931, he changed the organization's name from The Watch Tower Society to "Jehovah's Witnesses" based on Isaiah 43:10, "You are my witnesses." His total control of the organization enabled him to discard some of Russell's more unattractive teachings. Rutherford initiated the door-to-door visitation program and served as president until his death in 1942. (The Society's own biased version of its history is found in *Jehovah's Witnesses in the Divine Purpose.*)

Nathan H. Knorr followed Rutherford as president in 1942. His outreach methods increased the membership from 115,000 to over 2 million. He brought the organization through a trying time in 1975 when predictions were made that the world would end. Knorr died in 1977 and was followed by Frederick W. Franz, vice-president under him. In 1980, Franz struggled to hold the organization together when top leaders held opposing theological positions and were disfellowshiped at Bethel Headquarters. Among those was Franz' own nephew, Raymond Franz.

Knorr was considered by Jehovah's Witnesses to be the Society's most knowledgeable Hebrew scholar. However, he admitted under oath in a court trial in 1954 that he could not translate a simple verse, Genesis 2:24, back into Hebrew. At the time, he represented the translation committee for the Jehovah's Witnesses unique translation of the Bible, *The New World Translation.*[4]

The president of the Jehovah's Witnesses wields absolute control over its followers and over the doctrine of the movement. Such strict control over adherents is a chief mark of all cultic groups. The president has the power to make divine pronouncements, which are to be believed and followed without question.

The Brooklyn headquarters is known as Bethel. Witnesses who disagree with the leadership are disfellowshipped, or excommunicated. From that point on, Kingdom Hall worshipers and family members consider them dead and are forbidden to speak to them. The "apostate" is told he will not rise from the grave on Judgment Day.[5]

Out With the Old, in With the New

Every pseudo-Christian group has the same problem —the Bible. What are they to do with the Bible, since their beliefs are contrary to Scripture? The answer is to offer a new interpretation of the Bible. The Jehovah's Witnesses have actually taken upon themselves to rewrite the Bible to fit their theology. Such action insinuates that their scholars and interpreters are greater than scholars William Tyndale and John Wycliffe, the hundreds of scholars who gave us the King James Version, and the modern translators.

However, not one known Biblical scholar with recognized degrees in Hebrew or Greek exegesis or translation, served on the committee that produced *The New World Translation of the Holy Scripture* (1961). The translating team consisted of only five men. The contradictions between their translation and the Bible are well documented. Their desire to depart from orthodox Christian beliefs is evident by the fact that they sought a new translation at all.[6]

The translators of the *New World Translation* are anonymous, so neither credentials nor their manuscript source can be verified. But the inconsistencies between it and the King James Version are glaringly obvious. Anthony A. Hoekema, in *The Four Major Cults,* correctly points out that the "*New World Translation* is by no means an objective rendering of the sacred text into modern English, but is a biased translation in which many of the peculiar teachings of the Watchtower Society are smuggled into the text of the Bible itself."[7]

Here are a few examples among many:

1. *John 1:1 reads: "In the beginning was the Word, and the Word was with God, and the Word was God."* The Word (*logos*, Greek) is Jesus, the son of God. John the apostle emphatically affirms the divinity of Jesus, "the Word was God." The *New World Translation,* however, inserts the article "a" making it read, "the word was *a* god." Such mistranslating robs Christ of His divinity, which is the cornerstone of the Christian faith.

2. *John 8:58 reads: "'I tell you the truth,' Jesus answered, 'before Abraham was born, I am!'"* In their original footnote, they stated that this is the correct translation according to the perfect indefinite tense of the verb. Later, they changed it to the perfect tense so that Jesus says, "I have been" instead of "I am," which, of course, is Jesus' claim of divinity.

Actually, the verb is in the present tense in the Greek and correctly reads, "I am." In fact, from John 8:42 through 9:12 the verb "to be" (*eimi,* Greek) is used 21 times. The *New World Translation* correctly translates the verb tense 20 out of the 21 uses. Only in John 8:58 is it changed to fit their theology and to deny the deity of Jesus Christ.

3. *Colossians 1:15 reads: "He is the image of the invisible God, the firstborn over all creation."* The *New World Translation* changes "firstborn" to "first-created," in an effort to teach that Jesus is not divine, but rather a creation of God. But Paul the apostle goes on to say, "For by him (that is, Jesus) all things were created . . . all things were created by him and for him. He is before all things (that is, created things), and in him all things hold together" (Colossians 1:16, 17, parenthesis added).

The word *firstborn* means "to have preeminence; to be first in authority," not in creation. Further, the *New World Translation* adds the word "other" in the text: "He is before all [other] things." They put the word in brackets, which are said to "enclose words inserted to complete or clarify the sense of the English" (Foreword to the *New World Translation*).[8]

But they intentionally added the word *other* so as to make Christ part of creation and to strip Him of His deity. The verse reads clearly, "He is before all things," revealing the deity of Christ and His work in Creation. He is not a creation of God, He is the Creator, one with God the Father in creating all things. Paul goes on to declare the deity of Christ in this passage: "For God was pleased to have all his fullness dwell in him. . . . For in Christ all the fullness of the Deity lives in bodily form" (Colossians 1:19; 2:9).

4. *The Society claims to have restored the name Jehovah to the Biblical text.* The Witnesses say that Jehovah is the only name for God. (The pronunciation of Jehovah first appeared in William Tyndale's English translation of the Bible in the 1500s). However, the Hebrew Old Testament uses several names for God, all of which reveal the nature of God. Names such as Elohim, "the strong One, the Creator"; El Shaddai, "the Almighty" or literally "the God of the mountain"; and Adonai, "Lord, Ruler and Sovereign" are meaningful names of God. However, Yahweh, or Jehovah, as it is more commonly pronounced, is the special covenant name of God.

The name Jehovah appears 6,800 times in the Old Testament. When Jehovah is used in English translations, it is distinguished by small capitals letters, LORD. The name is probably pronounced Yahweh. It is a translation of the Hebrew name YHWH. This abbreviation is called the "tetragrammaton." The name was so sacred the ancient Israelites would not speak it. For centuries, the Hebrew language was written without vowels, hence the spelling YHWH. Since the vowels were added many years later, the original pronunciation is unknown.

Whether we say Yahweh or Jehovah, we are simply making an attempt to properly pronounce the name. I point this out because the Witnesses place so much emphasis on their belief that Jehovah is the only name of God. This simply is not the case.

5. *Matthew 27:50 reads: "And when Jesus had cried out again in a loud voice, he gave up his spirit."* This passage speaks of the death of Jesus on the cross. The word *spirit* is *pneuma* in the Greek New Testament. Yet, the *New World Translation* alters the statement to read, he "yielded up his breath." Why the play on words? Walter Martin observes that the Society wants it to appear that "Jesus only stopped breathing and did not yield up His invisible nature upon dying."

Jehovah's Witnesses do not believe the spirit survives beyond death. For them, death is the end of life and the end of the human soul, until the Resurrection. They intentionally substituted the word "breath" for spirit in order to change the meaning of Scripture and indoctrinate the reader.[9]

But Jesus' prayer of committal, "Father, into your hands I commit my spirit" (Luke 23:46), clearly reveals that the human spirit returns to God, and is fully alive and conscious in eternity at the moment of physical death. The *New World Translation* gets caught in its own trap of

141

changing the meaning of Biblical words to fit their misguided beliefs. They actually translate Luke 23:46 correctly, "And Jesus called with a loud voice and said: 'Father, into your hands I entrust my spirit.'" There was simply no way they could mistranslate the word *pneuma* on this verse and get by with it.

The Pen Is Mightier Than the Sword

According to Edmond C. Gruss, Jehovah's Witnesses can study the Bible using only the Watchtower publications. Two topically arranged Bible-verse handbooks (with verses frequently out of context) were designed to assist Witnesses in their Bible study: *Make Sure of All Things* (1953) and *Make Sure of All Things: Hold Fast to What Is Fine* (1965).[10] Such theological control keeps adherents from thinking outside the box of the Society's biased views.

Judge Rutherford, in his book *Creation,* writes concerning Charles Russell: "As William Tyndale was used to bring the Bible to the attention of the people, so the Lord used Charles T. Russell to bring to the attention of the people an understanding of the Bible, particularly of those truths that had been taken away by the machinations of the Devil and his agencies."[11]

The Jehovah's Witness movement seeks to influence through the power of the printed page. Judge Rutherford was a prolific writer who authored over 100 books and pamphlets, which by 1941 had been translated into 80 languages. *The Watchtower* is the centerpiece of Jehovah's Witnesses literature used to recruit new members and to indoctrinate existing ones.

142

The Watchtower Bible and Tract Society, the governing body of Jehovah's Witnesses, claims to be God's "collective channel for the flow of Biblical truth to men on earth in these last days" (*The Watchtower,* July 15, 1960). But Jesus promised His followers, "When . . . the Spirit of truth, comes, he will guide you into all truth" (John 16:13). Such revelation of Scripture is the ministry of the Holy Spirit and is promised to every believer.

The Holy Trinity

Jehovah's Witnesses deny all essential Christian doctrines. First, they deny the Holy Trinity. They like to point out that one of the predominant Trinitarian verses of the New Testament does not appear in many of the early manuscripts. First John 5:7, reads, "Three are who are testifying [in the heaven, the Father, the Word, and the Holy Spirit, and these—the three—are one]" (*Young's Literal Translation*). While it is true that this verse does not appear in early manuscripts, it does appear in later ones. Translators added it to complement what the apostle John was writing in the passage.

The fact remains, however, that the doctrine of the Trinity is predominant in Scripture. Baptism itself is to be administered "in the name of the Father and of the Son and of the Holy Spirit" (Matthew 28:19). Jesus prayed to the Father and spoke often of the ministry of the Holy Spirit (see John 14:16, 17). The Trinity is clearly portrayed in the baptism of Jesus in the Jordan River by John the Baptist (see Matthew 3:16, 17).

Christians do not believe, as falsely reported by the Society, in three gods. We believe in one God, eternally existing in three persons, who are coexistent, co-eternal and coequal. This is the mystery of the Holy Trinity.

Jesus, the Son of God

Jehovah's Witnesses deny the deity of Jesus as the son of God. They claim that Jesus is the first son that Jehovah brought forth but is not Jehovah God, nor one with Him. Further, they claim that Michael the archangel is Jesus. They acknowledge that Jesus has a pre-human existence and that He was born of the Virgin Mary.

According to the Society, Jesus was raised from the dead as a mighty immortal spirit; not a flesh body, but a spirit body. They deny the physical resurrection of Jesus from death. The *Watchtower* says that the body of Christ, which was crucified, was either dissolved into gases or is preserved in heaven as a memorial.

However, the physical, triumphant resurrection of Jesus from death is the cornerstone of the Christian faith and the hope of eternal life. When the risen Lord appeared to His frightened disciples, he asked, "Why are you troubled, and why do doubts rise in your minds? Look at my hands and my feet. It is I myself! Touch me and see; a ghost does not have flesh and bones, as you see I have" (Luke 24:38, 39).

His resurrection forms the foundation of the believer's assurance of resurrection and eternal life. Paul declares, "But our citizenship is in heaven. And we eagerly await a Savior from there, the Lord Jesus Christ, who, by the power that enables him to bring everything under his control, will transform our lowly bodies so that they will be like his glorious body" (Philippians 3:20, 21).

Another point of error in their doctrine concerns the Atonement of Christ. The forgiveness of sins is based on the universal atonement provided by the death of Christ on the cross. Yet, the Jehovah's Witness deny the eternal atonement of Christ. The Bible is clear that it is the blood of Christ that makes Atonement (Hebrews 9:22; 1 Peter 1:18- 20; 1 John 1:7).

They claim that atonement is not totally the work of God, but half is of God and half of man. Jesus "removed the effects of Adam's sin by His sacrifice on Calvary, but the work will not be fully completed until the survivors of Armageddon return to God through free will and become subject to the Theocratic rule of Jehovah."[12] Furthermore, Witnesses claim that Adam is not included in the redeemed, since he forfeited a perfect human life.

The Society claims that Jesus was not crucified on a cross but on a torture stake. They do not embrace the symbol of the cross. But Paul the apostle declared, "The message of the cross is foolishness to those who are perishing, but to us who are being saved it is the power of God" (1 Corinthians 1:18). "May I never boast except in the cross of our Lord Jesus Christ" (Galatians 6:14).

Born Again?

The Society does not teach that the new birth is necessary to obtain salvation. They claim that only the 144,000 are "born again" and will live in heaven. The rest will rise from the grave to live on the earth, so there is no need in being born again. But Jesus said, "No one can see the kingdom of God unless he is born again. . . .You must be born again" (John 3:3, 7).

Witnesses fail to understand the new birth. In their book *Make Sure of All Things,* they assert: "Born again means a birth-like realization of prospects and hopes for spirit life by resurrection to heaven. Such a realization is brought about through the water of God's truth in the Bible and God's holy spirit, his active force."[13]

But the New Testament clearly teaches that we are born again through repentance of sin and faith in Jesus Christ as Lord. The new birth means a total spiritual transformation from sin to righteousness, from darkness to light, from death to life. The new birth means a new creation: "The old has gone, the new has come!" (2 Corinthians 5:17).

We are born again through faith in Jesus Christ (John 3:7-16). The new birth guarantees every believer, not just the 144,000, entrance into the kingdom of God and ever-lasting life in heaven. Witnesses are known for using Biblical terms with entirely different meanings, so as to mislead their potential candidates.

When Christ Returns

The Jehovah's Witnesses deny Christ's promise to return to earth visibly and victoriously. Since He did not rise physically, they say, He will not return physically. The Society claims that Jesus returned in 1914 and that He reigns in an invisible realm, enacting the power of his kingdom through the Jehovah's Witnesses organization.

They maintain, "Christ has turned his attention toward earth's affairs and is dividing the peoples and educating the true Christians in preparation for their survival during the great storm of Armageddon, when all unfaithful mankind will be destroyed from the face of the earth."[14] For Jehovah's Witnesses, then, Jesus is not coming—He's already here!

Such a claim deserves a response from the Lord himself: "At that time if anyone says to you, 'Look, here is the Christ!' or, 'There he is!' do not believe it. For false Christs and false prophets will appear and . . . deceive even the elect—if that were possible" (Matthew 24:23, 24).

The same false teaching went around in the early church. The apostle Paul confronted it head-on:

Concerning the coming of our Lord Jesus Christ and our being gathered to him, we ask you, brothers, not to become easily unsettled or alarmed by some prophecy, report or letter supposed to have come from us, saying that the day of the Lord has already come. Don't let anyone deceive you in any way, for that day will not come until the rebellion occurs and the man of lawlessness (the Antichrist) is revealed, the man doomed to destruction (2 Thessalonians 2:1-3, parentheses added).

When Christ returns, the whole world will see Him in the fullness of His glory and power. Yet their book *The Truth Shall Make You Free* claims, "It is a settled Scriptural truth . . . that human eyes will not see him at his second coming, neither will he appear in a fleshly body."[15] The *New World Translation* repeatedly mistranslates the Greek word *parousia*, which is used by the apostles to describe the

147

appearing or the return of Christ. They consistently translate *parousia* as "presence" instead of "coming," or "appearing," so they can justify the nonsense that Christ returned invisibly in 1914.

But the Revelator exclaims, "Look, he is coming with the clouds, and every eye will see him, even those who pierced him; and all the peoples of the earth will mourn because of him. So shall it be! Amen" (Revelation 1:7). His *parousia* will not be an invisible, secretive return, but a grand entrance of cosmic proportions!

A study of the Society's teachings of the end times reveals their confusion. The world's end has been foretold for 1914, 1918, 1920, 1925, 1941 and 1975. An interesting mathematical system is used for setting the date of the world's end at Armageddon. They teach that Adam was created in 4026 B.C. Witnesses taught that the 6,000 years of human history would end in 1975. When 1975 passed without Armageddon happening, thousands of disillusioned members left the cult. But President Franz explained that the 6,000 year chronology began with Eve's creation not Adam's.[16]

The *Watchtower* reads: "Does this mean that we know exactly when God will destroy this old system and establish a new one? Franz showed that we do not know how short was the time interval between Adam's creation and the creation of Eve, at which point God's rest day of seven thousand years began." But the interval between the creation of Adam and Eve has yet to be revealed by Witness' leaders. Still, they hold to the belief that the end is at hand.[17]

148

They teach that the last 1,000 years of human history and the millennial reign of Christ will coincide. The Revelation, however, teaches that Armageddon signals the beginning of the Millennium (see Revelation 19:11-16; 20:1-15). Needless to say, the Witnesses are very confused on the Biblical teaching of the last days. Supposedly, the 144,000 have been gathered into heaven since the return of Christ in 1914. Armageddon must occur and the Millennium begin before all the 144,000 "anointed class" from 1914 have died. Bob Larson reports that Witnesses believe "less that 10,000 of the 144,000 are left."[18]

The Holy Spirit: Person or Force?

Jesus taught that the Holy Spirit is a person. "And I will ask the Father, and he will give you another Counselor to be with you forever—the Spirit of truth. The world cannot accept him, because it neither sees him nor knows him. But you know him, for he lives with you and will be in you" (John 14:16, 17).

Jehovah's Witnesses view the Holy Spirit as God's invisible active force, which moves His servants to do His will. They emphatically claim that the Holy Spirit is not a person. But notice in these verses how Jesus repeatedly refers to the Holy Spirit as a Person.

The Christian life is lived in the power and presence of the Holy Spirit. The Holy Spirit is mentioned 261 times in the New Testament, as well as in numerous Old Testament references. The Holy Spirit is not an impersonal force, an emotional experience or a psychic phenomenon. He is God, third member of the Holy Trinity, who is coexistent, co-eternal and coequal with the Father and Son.

149

What does the Holy Spirit do in the world? He ministers the new birth to us (John 3:5-8); indwells believers (1 Corinthians 6:19); seals us for the day of redemption (Ephesians 1:13); guides us into all truth (John 16:13); assures us of salvation (Romans 8:15-17); intercedes with us in prayer (Romans 8:26, 27); empowers us for service (Luke 24:49); and convicts the world of sin and its need of the Savior (John 16:7-11).

Life After Death

Jehovah's Witnesses believe that all who by reason of faith in Jehovah God and in Christ Jesus dedicated themselves to do God's will and then faithfully carry out their dedication will be rewarded with everlasting life. However, they also teach that only the 144,000 go to heaven. The rest will be given eternal life on the earth, provided they remain faithful after the Battle of Armageddon and the final judgment.[19]

When a person dies, the soul (entire being) is unconscious and inactive. They teach that death means the cessation of the soul's existence. When the body dies, the soul dies with it and no longer exists. The publication *Make Sure of All Things,* defines death as follows: "Death—loss of life; termination of existence; utter cessation of consciousness; intellectual or physical activating, celestial, human or otherwise." [20]

There is no heaven for believers. When you die, you cease to exist. You then wait for God to recreate you at the end of the age on the day of resurrection. Hell is defined as the annihilation of the soul. Those who reject the kingdom message will be annihilated. This, they claim, is the lake of fire referred to in Revelation 20:11-15.

The Society teaches that the soul is merely a life force or principle that animates the body; it is not separate from the body. They deny the immaterial, spiritual nature of man which lives after the body dies. Concerning Christ's resurrection, they claim that God recreated Him as a spirit being, since no part of Him existed after His death. Faithful Witnesses have no hope of heaven. They hope to be recreated from Jehovah's mind and live on a perfected earth after Armageddon.[21]

The Bible clearly teaches the immortality of the soul. Ecclesiastes promises, "The dust returns to the ground it came from, and the spirit returns to God who gave it" (12:7). When a believers dies, his or her soul is instantly with Christ in heaven. Paul reflects on life after death: "For to me, to live is Christ and to die is gain. . . . I am torn between the two: I desire to depart and be with Christ, which is better by far; but it is more necessary for you that I remain in the body" (Philippians 1:21, 23, 24). He assures us, "as long as we are at home in the body we are away from the Lord. . . . We are confident, I say, and would prefer to be away from the body and at home with the Lord" (2 Corinthians 5:6, 8).

What could be any clearer on the subject of life after death than the words of Jesus?

"Do not let your hearts be troubled. Trust in God; trust also in me. In my Father's house are many rooms; if it were not so, I would have told you. I am going there to prepare a place for you. And if I go and prepare a place for

151

you, I will come back and take you to be with me that you also may be where I am" (John 14:1-3, emphasis added).

Where is Jesus? He is in heaven at the right hand of God, the Father (see Romans 8:34). Jesus promises every believer that he has prepared a special place for us in heaven with him for all eternity.

Other Key Beliefs

The Society rejects the celebration of birthdays, Christmas and Easter, which are deemed pagan in their origins. Each year in March, they hold a memorial service to commemorate Christ's sacrifice, which began the covenant between Jehovah and the 144,000. The meal is similar to Holy Communion, yet only a few partake even though it is considered to be purely symbolic. They ignore their estimated date for Christ's birth, October 2. The only birthday they celebrate is that of the Society itself, which celebrated its 100th birthday in 1984.

They reject the idea that the present gathering of the Jews in Israel is a fulfillment of Biblical prophecy. According to the Society, God only works with spiritual Israel. The Jehovah's Witnesses claim that the Bible cannot be understood apart from the teachings of the Society. They will not salute the flag, which is considered idolatrous. They also refuse to serve in the military.[22]

What Is Their Mission?

Unlike the Mormons, the conversion rate of Jehovah's Witnesses is slow. Today, the group's growth is slowing. With nearly a million active "publishers" (members) in the United States last year, the Witnesses baptized only 30,000 converts, down from a high of nearly 50,000 in 1988, according to statistics in the January 1, 2001 issue of the *Watchtower* magazine. Yet, they remain aggressive in their efforts.[23]

What, exactly, is their mission? Jehovah's Witnesses seek to usher in the messianic age at Armageddon. Since the 144,000 already sealed will remain in heaven with Christ, current-day Witnesses hope to live eternally on the new earth. Such fanatical views appeal to persons with an apocalyptic mentality who are preoccupied with the end of the age but who lack an understanding of Biblical teaching on the last days.

William J. Schnell, in *Thirty Years a Watch Tower Slave,* explains the Witnesses' 7-step plan for recruiting followers: (1) Get literature into the hands of people through door-to-door campaigns or other outreaches. (2) Follow up with a "back call" to encourage interest in the Society. (3) Try to schedule a "book study" using Watchtower materials. (4) Get interested persons to attend a corporate book study. (5) Bring those showing interest to a "Watchtower study." (6) Encourage attendance at the "service meeting" and the "Theocratic Ministry" school. (7) The last step is to dedicate oneself to Jehovah in baptism.[24]

Like all cults, control of members by the governing authority is a chief mark of the Society. Each Kingdom Hall indoctrinates its followers and stands ready to rebut any questions raised. Sharing your faith with Jehovah's Witnesses begins with showing love and respect for their views. Remember, they are programmed to hold their views. They haven't carefully examined them in light of the Bible, since they use an altered version of the Scripture designed to support the Society's teachings.

Help them think outside the box by focusing your discussions on the Bible. Draw their attention to what the Bible really teaches about such subjects as the new birth, eternal life for all believers, the immortality of the soul, the deity of Jesus Christ as the Son of God and the Savior of the world, and the kingdom of God of which every Christian is a part. Above all, share your personal testimony of salvation and the hope of eternal life that is yours.

Cultic activity, such as seen by the Jehovah's Witnesses, serves as a solemn challenge to believers to know the faith and to be on guard against spiritual deception. William J. Schnell offers such a challenge:

> The Watchtower leadership sense that within the midst of Christendom were millions of professing Christians who were not well-grounded in the truths once delivered to the saints, and who would rather easily be pried loose from the churches and led into a new and revitalized Watchtower organization. The Society calculated, and rightly, that this lack of proper knowledge of God and the widespread acceptance of half-truths in Christendom would yield vast masses of men and women, if wisely attacked, the attack sustained and the results contained, and then used in an ever-widening circle.[25]

"Be on your guard so that you may not be carried away by the error of lawless men and fall from your secure position. But grow in the grace and knowledge of our Lord and Savior Jesus Christ. To him be glory both now and forever! Amen" (2 Peter 3:17, 18).

In Search of Jesus

I got behind a car one day with an interesting bumper sticker: *If Jesus is the answer, what is the question?* The question is, *How can I find God?*

Americans are searching for God with renewed fervency, according to researchers George Gallup Jr. and Timothy Jones. In *The Next American Spirituality*, they report that Americans seem to be praying more, and increased interest in spiritual life is evident. Although church attendance is declining in some parts of the country and secularism continues to pervade public life, people are searching for God. "Spirituality is back almost with a vengeance," says Martin Marty, historian of modern religion.

Tragically, the sincere search for God ends up misguided for many. People aren't even sure what they mean by the term *spirituality,* even though they claim to be searching for spiritual fulfillment. According to Gallup and Jones, when faced with difficulty and discouragement, a majority of persons turn to "God, a higher power, the inner self, or Jesus Christ."[1]

The search for God ends when we meet Jesus Christ.

A Sunday school teacher noticed little Johnny drawing a picture of an old man during arts and crafts.

"Who's picture are you drawing?" she asked.

"I'm drawing a picture of God," he responded confidently.

"But no one has ever seen God. No one knows what God looks like," said the teacher.

Johnny replied, "Well, they will when I'm finished with this picture."

When Jesus came into the world, the world knew exactly what God looked like. When we see Jesus, God is no longer obscure. In Islam, God is Allah, the God who cannot be known. In strict Judaism, God is righteous law. The Pharisees of Jesus' day saw God as the lawgiver and judge. To the Buddhist, God is an impersonal spirit that permeates all creation. To the Hindu, God is truth and bliss. To the ancient Greeks, God is wisdom. To the humanist, God is the innate power of goodness within us. To the scientist, God is natural law.

But in Christianity, God is love.

Children have interesting insights on God. A little girl surprised her family during prayer time. After she finished praying for her family and herself, she added, "And now, God, what can I do for you?"

During the children's sermon, the minister asked a little boy, "Can you tell me who made you, Jimmy?"

"Well," he said, "God made part of me."

"What do you mean?" asked the preacher.

"God made me little and I growed the rest myself," Jimmy replied.

Have you ever noticed that every religion welcomes Jesus? I find this intriguing. No religion wants to exclude Jesus. I also find it interesting that everyone reveres Jesus. During the 60s a slogan became popular among the Jesus freaks: *Jesus, yes! Christianity, no!* Jesus is a big-time *yes!* in every religion.

What's so special about Him? Philip Yancey has written a terrific book titled *The Jesus I Never Knew.* Although raised in the church, his view of Jesus was quite skewed and erroneous. His insights on Jesus are refreshing. He gives two reasons why he is a Christian: First, because of the lack of good alternatives, and second, because of Jesus.

An unknown writer has captured the ageless impact of Jesus:

He was born in an obscure village. He worked in a carpenter's shop until He was 30. He then became an itinerant preacher. He never held an office. He never had a family or owned a house. He didn't go to college. He had no credentials but Himself. He was only 33 when the public turned against Him. His friends ran away. He was turned over to His enemies and went through the mockery of a trial. He was nailed to a cross between two thieves. While He was dying, His executioners gambled for His clothing, the only property He had on earth. He was laid in a borrowed grave. Twenty centuries have come and gone, and today He is the central figure of the human race. All the armies that ever marched, all the navies that ever sailed, all the parliaments that ever sat, and all the kings that ever reigned have not affected the life of man on this earth as much as that One Solitary Life.

Jesus Is Misunderstood

Today, many people follow a distorted image of Jesus. I don't remember the author who got me thinking about the misguided perspectives of Jesus, but they are worth noting.

There are those who worship the *sentimental Jesus*. They get emotional at Christmas, reflecting on the majesty of His birth in Bethlehem. They are stirred by Christmas pageants. But for them, Jesus remains wrapped in swaddling clothes, lying in a manger. He never gets out of the manger and into their hearts.

Some are preoccupied by their quest for the *historical Jesus*. They search through pages of antiquity and through archaeological ruins looking for historical evidence to confirm or deny His life, ministry, death and resurrection. To them, Jesus is an idea to be debated, a concept to be researched or an archaeological relic to be unearthed.

The *religious Jesus* is a beloved figure along with other religious leaders such as Buddha, Mohammed and Confucius. He is a prophet extraordinaire; the Incarnation of divine truth and love. Sadly, they keep him in a museum displayed with other leaders of days gone by.

The New Agers see Jesus as a *good man* who, through His good deeds and self-mastery, achieved what they call "Christhood." We too, according to them, can transcend human limitations through self-discovery and realize this same Christ potential that resides in us all.

The *ecclesiastical Jesus*, the Jesus of organized Christianity, is marred by the sins of church leaders and followers throughout history. He gets blamed for the Crusades, the Holocaust and televangelist scandals. Some people never get to Christ because they can't get beyond the failures and exploitations of some who claim His name.

There are those who follow the *moral Jesus*. They diligently study His teachings and moral principles, such as the Beatitudes and the Golden Rule. For them, Jesus remains entombed in a shrine of philosophical motifs. Jesus is admired and studied, but not applied.

Finally, there is the *cultic Jesus*. Frightening cults are everywhere. They distort Jesus to their own destruction. Thirty-nine people in Rancho Santa Fe, California, committed suicide as a part of a group that was called Heaven's Gate. Their leader, called Do (pronounced *Doe*), had told them Jesus was a space alien. He promised them that a spacecraft would receive them on the other side of the Hale-Bopp comet through a window opened by the comet, if they committed suicide. Tragically, they believed the lie.

Now, allow me to introduce you to the real Jesus.

JESUS, THE MAN

In his book *Mere Christianity*, C.S. Lewis says, "The Son of God became a man to enable men to become sons of God." What a miracle of miracles—the Son of God became a man.

When I read the Christmas narrative in the Gospel of Luke, I am fascinated with the simple phrase, "lying in a manger." What a strange, unassuming place to find God when He came to earth. You would expect the story to report something like, "lying in a palace, in the splendor of royalty." But lying in a manger?

The only sight greater than God in a manger is God on a cross.

I'm sure you've found consolation in talking to someone who understood your experience because they had had a similar experience. When we go through grief, there is a feeling that we're the only ones going through it. But Jesus has been where you are. He understands what you feel and what you are going through with your struggles.

Jesus not only came to reveal God to us, He also came to show us what it means to be truly human. Irenaeus said, "The glory of God is a human being who is fully alive." Never is that statement truer than in the humanity of Jesus.

One of the most inspiring books I've ever read is entitled, *Who Is This Jesus?* by Michael Green. His insights into the humanity of Jesus are incredible. Using his insights and adding some of my own, I want to introduce you to Jesus, the man.[2]

Jesus Was an Enjoyable Person to Be Around

People enjoyed His company. He was pleasant, humorous, self-assured and secure. He loved people and loved life. He lived with a great sense of balance. I see so many people whose spiritual life is at a fever-pitched level. You never see Jesus like that in Scripture. Jesus could mingle with intellectuals and commoners alike. He could converse with theologians and lawyers, yet talk to children. He was no respecter of persons. He was happy and joyful. He was a man for all men.

Jesus Made God Real

He is "the image of the invisible God" (Colossians 1:15). People saw a different God in Jesus than they saw in the prevailing religious mood of the day. Jesus spoke of God as our Father. He made God accessible and attractive. They felt close to God when they were with Jesus.

Jesus Lived a Model Life For All To Follow

People today are looking for role models. We look to actors, Hollywood stars and athletes. Jesus is the role model we need. His invitation was simply, "Follow me." He is a person we can follow. We can follow everything about Him. He was the epitome of a role model for children and the pattern of true success for all to emulate. No one has ever lived as He lived. He lived a life of utmost integrity. He was sinless.

And He didn't mind getting His hands dirty with human problems. On one occasion, He touched a leper and made him clean. Some say that God cannot look upon sin. Not only can Jesus look at us in our sin, He will touch us and make us whole.

Jesus Was Merciful and Kind

He was a source of inexhaustible mercy. If you were to ask me what quality is most attractive to me about Jesus, I would say, "His mercy." He intervened for an adulterous woman who faced execution by stoning. He fed a hungry multitude when the disciples thought the people should get their own food. He spent time with a Samaritan woman who was a social outcast.

161

He invited drunkards, tax collectors and prostitutes to enter the kingdom of God. He took time out of His schedule for little children. He forgave His enemies as He hung on a cross. He pictured love as a father who patiently waited for his prodigal son to come home and then restored him to his full inheritance.

Jesus' Teaching Was Incomparable

The scribes and teachers of Christ's day constantly relied on the words of great men to back up their teachings. But not Jesus; He quoted no one. He had no footnotes in His messages. His word was the very Word of God. What about our words? If we are to follow Him, let us speak as He spoke—with words that will change the course of history.

Jesus Was Completely Free

Freedom is the greatest human experience. We cherish freedom in America and are the envy of the world because we are so free. But Jesus possessed an even greater freedom. He was free from worry, anxiety and concern. "Do not worry," He often told His followers.

He was also free from legalism. He read the Old Testament but thought outside the box of tradition. He was free from social prejudice. He was free from the opinions of others. He was free from their praise when they wanted to make Him king. And He was free from their ridicule when they called Him a glutton, drunkard and blasphemer. Jesus knew who He was and no one could shake His confidence.

Jesus Lived Life With Purpose

His highest aspiration was to do the will of His Father. "Not my will, but yours be done," was his prayer in the face of death (Luke 22:42). He didn't drift aimlessly. He didn't react to circumstances. He was proactive. He was on a mission. His last words were, "It is finished" (John 19:30).

Jesus Rose Above Suffering

He experienced the unfathomable depths of human suffering. He felt pain, loss and grief. He was a man of sorrows, He was acquainted with grief. He wept at the grave of His friend, Lazarus. He knew what it was like to be misunderstood, rejected and even hated. Yet, He transcended suffering. He suffered the cruelty of crucifixion. Even then He trusted God, as He prayed, "Father, into your hands I commit my spirit" (Luke 23:46).

Jesus possessed a triumphant attitude when faced with adversity. "In the world you will have tribulation," He told His disciples, "but be of good cheer, I have overcome the world" (John 16:33, *NKJV*). He was always a victor, never a victim.

Jesus' Love Was and Is Universal

He never met a person He didn't love. Jesus was the incarnation of love. His love was unconditional. His love was sacrificial. He laid down His life for us. No one ever taught about love as Jesus did. Love for God and one's neighbor is the greatest commandment and the bottom line of true religion, according to Jesus. Love is the law of His kingdom (John 13:34, 35).

163

The single most moving scene of Christ's life was His crucifixion. Above the cries of agony, rose the shout of His love—"Father, forgive them, for they do not know what they are doing" (Luke 23:34). What amazing love!

I counseled a woman in our congregation who was concerned about the spiritual condition of her employer. The man struggles with intellectual objections to the gospel of Christ. Yet he told her he feels spiritually empty.

"How can I share my faith with him?" she asked. "I can't answer all his intellectual objections to the gospel of Christ."

She asked me to recommend some books that deal with intellectual objections to the faith. I told her that while such books serve a useful purpose (and recommended several to her), the most powerful witness she could give her employer is her personal experience of faith. I told her, "Just go to him and ask him if he will allow you to share with him what Jesus means to you."

My point is—Jesus is captivating. He always has been and always will be. No one who has come into contact with the risen Christ can deny the power of a changed life.

For almost 18 years Dian Fossey, a California-born zoologist, worked with gorillas on the continent of Africa. Working in the Virunga Mountains located in Rwanda, she isolated herself from civilization to learn the ways of gorillas. She first visited Africa in 1963. In 1967 she returned to Africa to study rare mountain gorillas in Rwanda. The gorillas accepted her. She saw the creatures as deserving of her love. She identified with them, cared for their newborn, cried with them when they mourned their dead and even named them. She wrote:

These powerful but shy and gentle animals accepted and responded to my attentions when I acted like a gorilla. So I learned to scratch and groom and beat my chest. I imitated my subjects' vocalizations (hoots, grunts and belches), munched the foliage they ate, kept low to the ground and deliberate in movement.[3]

After 18 years with the gorillas, the place was home. She had made her home with them, she became like them, she dwelt among them, they were her friends. When faced with the danger of her mission, she refused to leave. In 1985, she died among those she went to save. Apparently, she was murdered by poachers whose trade she sought to destroy.

What a graphic parallel to illustrate why Jesus came into the world. Paul summed it up best: "Christ Jesus came into the world to save sinners—of whom I am the worst" (1 Timothy 1:15).

JESUS, THE DIVINE

Now that we have met Jesus the man, let's look at His divinity. To say that Jesus is divine is to say that He is God—one with the Father. Here lies the dividing line between Christianity and other religions. People want to stop short of saying that Jesus is divine. But if Jesus is not divine, then He is merely a man like us who has no power to save us.

What did Jesus say about Himself? There is no mistaking the fact that Jesus openly claimed to be the Son of God. On the night of the Passover, Jesus made a statement, which has since become the most powerful, yet controversial,

165

statement He made: "I am the way and the truth and the life. No one comes to the Father except through me. If you really knew me, you would know my Father as well. From now on, you do know him and have seen him" (John 14:6, 7).

As you can imagine, this led to an intriguing discussion among the disciples. Philip said to him, "Lord, show us the Father and that will be enough for us" (v. 8).

Sounds like us, doesn't it? Who has not prayed at one time or another to see God, at least in a dream or a vision? We all want to see God. Now, listen to Jesus' response to his request and to ours:

> Don't you know me, Philip, even after I have been among you such a long time? Anyone who has seen me has seen the Father. How can you say, "Show us the Father?" Don't you believe that I am in the Father, and that the Father is in me? The words I say to you are not just my own. Rather, it is the Father, living in me, who is doing his work (vv. 9, 10).

Faith begins with the dynamic discovery of who Jesus really is. On one occasion, Jesus posed the question to His disciples: "'Who do you say I am?' Simon Peter answered, 'You are the Christ, the Son of the living God'" (Matthew 16:15, 16).

Because Jesus is divine, He is greater than any other religious figure in human history. In fact, no other leader ever claimed to be divine—not Confucius, Buddha or Mohammed. Jesus' claim to be divine is as unique as His offer of salvation.

Let's be clear on this vital truth. Jesus is not just a good man who attained a level of divinity or oneness with the universe because of His spiritual enlightenment. Such notions about Jesus are prominent in other religions. The Christian faith asserts undauntedly that Jesus is God, who came to earth in the form of humanity.

The entire Christian faith rests on the foundation of the deity of Jesus. This is why we say that Jesus is the only way to God. Thomas Aquinas expounded on Jesus' claim:

> I am the Way, the Truth, and the Life. Without the way, no journey can be taken. Without the truth, no truth can be known. Without the life, no life can be lived. I am the Way which must be followed; I am the Truth which must be believed; I am the Life for which man must hope.

Jesus did not claim to be *a* way to God; He claimed to be *the* way—the only way. The concept of "the way" is also predominant in other religions. Buddha claimed to be the discoverer of a lost, forgotten way. Confucius called his teaching *Tao*, the Way. Philo called philosophy, "The Royal Way."

Jesus declared, "I am the way." He does not say, "I show you the way," or "I teach you the way," but "I am the way." The early Christians simply called themselves *The Way* (see Acts 9:2; 19:9).

Jesus' claim to be *The Way* reminds me of the difference between giving directions to a person who is lost as opposed to actually leading him to his destination. I was getting gasoline one day when a couple pulled their car next to mine and asked directions to Highway 41. After

167

giving them directions, I realized they were still confused about where to go. So I said, "Follow me." They followed behind my car until I led them to their destination.

Jesus is the way to what or whom? He is the way to God. Jesus came to earth for one reason—to reconcile us to God by saving us from sin.

Jerome was an influential church leader who translated the Latin Vulgate version of the Bible around A.D. 400. He wanted people to be able to read the Bible in their own language. He was living in Bethlehem, where he worked on his translation. Toward the end of his life, he tells of having a dream of the Christ child.

In his dream, he was overwhelmed with reverence and awe just as were the Magi. He too wanted to give a gift. He offered the Christ child money but Jesus said, "I don't want it." Jerome gathered all his prized possessions and offered them as a gift, but again the Christ child said, "I don't want them."

"What, then, can I give you?" Jerome asked.

The Christ child said, "Give me your sin. That's what I came for."

Why People Reject Jesus

A verse in John's Gospel troubles me deeply. John writes beautifully about Jesus, whom he calls the Word, coming into the world. "He was in the world, and though the world was made through him, the world did not recognize him. He came to that which was his own, but his own did not receive him" (John 1:10, 11).

John does not mean merely that Christ came to the Jewish people when he speaks of those who were the Savior's own people. Many of the Jews did believe in him, as did many Gentiles. He meant humanity in general did not receive Him. Why do people reject Jesus and His invitation to believe in Him as their Savior and Lord?

There are those who reject Jesus because they say, *I don't need a Savior.* They are content with their own scientific, objective view of reality and don't need religion. Like Karl Marx, they believe religion is a crutch. While preaching, Billy Graham quoted Marx and said, "I agree. Religion is a crutch. But who's not limping?"

Some people deny the existence of God or of moral absolutes. For them, sin is a myth based on the illusion of religion. Or, they believe that their eternal state will depend on whether or not their good works outweigh their evil deeds.

Humanists believe man is basically good, not evil. So, who needs a Savior? Humanists believe that we need a better environment to bring out our innate goodness—not redemption. We aren't sinners, they claim, we are basically good people who have been corrupted by a bad environment. They claim that our problem is external not internal; social and not spiritual.

But who created the bad environment? We did. Jesus said, "Out of men's hearts, come . . . theft, murder, adultery" (Mark 7:21). The condition of the human heart creates the cultural environment. While we do have a good side to our nature, there is also something fundamentally wrong with our makeup. The Bible calls it sin. Every person is terminal with the disease of sin. And only the grace of God can cure us of its penalty and power.

169

Others reject Jesus because they equate him with *those who extort the gospel*. True, there have been those who have advanced their armies in His name and committed atrocious acts against humanity. But such acts as the Crusades were not the acts of true Christians but of those who manipulated the name of Christ for their own agenda. Can we honestly lay such sins at the feet of Jesus?

Then, there is *the problem of hypocrisy*. Supposedly, Gandhi was asked by a friend, "If you are so intrigued with Jesus Christ, why don't you become a Christian?"

Gandhi replied, "When I meet a Christian who is a follower of Christ, I might consider it."

I'm confident Gandhi did meet those who were insincere Christians. But I am equally confident that he met many authentic Christians. He certainly knew the great missionary, E. Stanley Jones, who had a profound impact on Gandhi for Christ.

People today still reject Jesus because His followers don't always live up to their claims. However, Jesus never said, "Follow my followers." He said, "Follow me."

Some reject Jesus because they *deny history,* suggesting instead that Jesus never actually lived. For them, Jesus was a figment of the imagination of early Christians. But the historical evidence for Jesus is undeniable. Michael Green in *Who Is This Jesus?* makes the case for the historical Jesus.[4]

Tacitus was a great Roman historian. In the year A.D. 115, he wrote a careful record of major events under each emperor on a yearly basis. He wrote an interesting account concerning the year A.D. 64, the year the great fire engulfed the city of Rome. He concurs with the prevailing view of the people that Emperor Nero was responsible for the fire because he wanted to rebuild the city for his own renown. Listen to what Tacitus recorded about Jesus:

> To dispel the rumor, Nero substituted as culprits and treated with the most extreme punishments, some people, popularly known as Christians, whose disgraceful activities were notorious. The originator of the name, Christ, had been executed when Tiberius was emperor by order of the procurator Pontius Pilate. But the deadly cult, though checked for a time, was now breaking out not only in Judea, the birthplace of this evil, but even throughout Rome. . . . (Annal 15.44).

It is obvious that Tacitus was no friend of Christianity, but he did get his history right. He records that Christ was born in Judea and lived in the reign of Tiberius (A.D. 14-37), was executed by Pilate (who governed the province A.D. 26-36), and had an influential following of disciples.

A contemporary of Tacitus was Pliny the Younger who was sent to govern Bythnia (northern Turkey) in A.D. 112. He was a power-hungry politician who was always writing letters to Emperor Trajan. He wrote a long letter about Christians when Christianity was spreading like wildfire in his province. Pagan temples were closing down for lack of worshipers, Roman sacred festivals were poorly attended, and the demand for sacrificial animals had all but dried up due to the massive conversions of so many Romans. Pliny executed those who confessed faith in Jesus and openly admitted doing so.

In this letter he attests to the utmost integrity of Christians in their services. The only cause for their execution was their refusing to practice emperor worship. He records that they met on Sundays to sing hymns to Christ as God. He says their lives were exemplary. You would not find fraud, adultery, theft or dishonesty among them. And at their common meal they ate food of ordinary and innocent kind, probably a reference to the Lord's Supper. While Pliny says nothing directly about Jesus, he does document the widespread influence of Christianity and its phenomenal power.

Flavius Josephus was a guerrilla commander in the war against Rome between A.D. 66 and 70. After the war, he became a historian and wrote in an effort to restore the dignity of the Jews in the eyes of the Romans. He wrote about the Herods; Caiaphas, the high priest; John the Baptist; and James, "the brother of Jesus, so-called Christ"—all names familiar to us in the New Testament. He writes an extensive piece on Jesus himself:

> And there arose about this time (that is, Pilate's time, A.D. 26-36) Jesus as a wise man, if indeed one should call him a man, For he was the performer of astonishing deeds, a teacher of those who are happy to receive the truth. He won over many Jews, and also many Greeks. He was the Christ (or Messiah). In response, to a charge presented by the leading men among us, Pilate condemned him to the cross but those who had loved him at first did not give up. For he appeared to them on the third day alive again as the holy prophets had foretold and had said many other wonderful things about him. And still to this day the race of Christians, named after him, has not died out (Antiquities 18:3.3).

Then, there are those who reject Jesus by saying, *I'm not good enough to follow Jesus*. I meet a lot of people like this. Their guilt keeps them from Christ. The good news is that Jesus said He did not come into this world to call the righteous, but the sinners to repentance. There is only one condition necessary to come to Jesus—you have to be a sinner. If you can admit that, you can be forgiven.

Frederick the Great once toured a prison in Berlin. As he walked along the rows of cells, the prisoners fell to their knees, beseeching him to pardon them. They all proclaimed their innocence, except for one man who remained silent. Frederick had the silent man brought to him. He asked, "Why are you here?"

The man answered, "Robbery."

Frederick said, "Are you guilty?"

The man paused for a moment, hung his head then answered, "Yes, Sire, I am. I am guilty and deserve the punishment I'm receiving."

The king ordered the man to be released immediately. He granted him a full pardon. The man thanked the king repeatedly and asked why he was granting him his freedom.

Frederick said, "You are a guilty man. I will not have you in this prison corrupting these fine, innocent people who occupy it."

Finally, people reject Jesus because *they feel they have made such a mess of their lives.* What would Jesus possibly want with them? Jesus is in the business of restoring broken lives. Just read the Gospels and see the kind of characters Jesus called to be His disciples. You've probably got a lot in common with that motley crew, and so do I. It is said of Jesus, "While in the company of sinners, He dreamed of saints." Jesus sees your potential as a saint.

173

Some years ago in Scotland, a couple of men spent the day fishing. That evening they were having dinner in a local inn when one got carried away describing the size of a fish he caught. He flung his hands and hit the cup of tea the waitress was about to put on the table. The cup dashed against the wall, leaving an ugly brown stain.

The fisherman apologized. Another customer came over to the table and said, "Don't worry about it." Sir Edwin Landseer, England's foremost painter of animals, took a pen from his pocket and began sketching a beautiful royal stag with antlers spread, around the ugly stain. So Jesus replaces the ugly stains in our lives with a beautiful work of art.

Who Needs a Savior?

What is the difference between Jesus and other religious leaders such as Buddha, Mohammed, Confucius, or others? That's simple—the other religious leaders were all men looking for truth. Jesus is the truth!

A number of years ago, a Christian leader named C.K. Lee lectured at American universities. He told the students how desperately China needed Jesus. After one lecture, a student asked Mr. Lee, "Why do you say that China needs Jesus? You have the teachings of Confucius."

Lee replied, "China needs Jesus for three reasons. First, Confucius is a teacher; Christ is a Savior. China needs a savior more than she needs a teacher. Second, Confucius is dead, but Christ is alive. China needs a living Savior. Third, one day Confucius will meet Christ as Judge. China needs to know Christ as Savior before she meets him as Judge."

The name *Jesus* means Savior. The entire message of Christianity is wrapped up in that one word—salvation. All religions have three things in common—beliefs, worship and a code of conduct. Only Christianity promises salvation.

Steven Spielberg's movie *Saving Private Ryan* tells the story of an Army captain named John Miller (played by Tom Hanks). In the aftermath of the D-Day invasion at Normandy Beach in World War II, Captain Miller receives orders to locate a private among thousands of displaced soldiers. He is to return Private James F. Ryan to his mother, whose other three sons have been killed in action.

Captain Miller and the small group of men assigned to help him successfully locate Ryan but then are forced to defend a strategic bridge against German tanks and troops. Captain Miller is fatally wounded in the attack. In his dying moments, he reaches out to Ryan, who holds him in his arms, and says, "Earn this! Earn this!"

Years later Ryan stands at the grave of Miller and wonders aloud if he has indeed earned the right to live.

Two thousand years ago Jesus died on the cross that we might live forever. His final words to us were not, "Earn this!" But rather, "It is finished. Receive this . . . as a free gift."

Before we discuss world religions any further, let me ask you, have you received Jesus Christ as your Savior? I am sure some who will read this book are still searching for God.

Your search can end now if you will put your faith in Jesus Christ. Jesus said, "God so loved the world that he gave his one and only Son, that whoever believes in him shall not perish but have eternal life" (John 3:16).

First, *acknowledge that Jesus is who He claimed to be—the Son of God.* Say, "Jesus, I believe that you are the Christ, the son of the living God."

Next, *trust Christ to save you from your sins.* You cannot save yourself. You cannot forgive your own sins. Only Christ can save you for eternity. You have to depend on Him to do for you what you cannot do for yourself.

Finally, *surrender your life to Jesus as Lord.* Give up the right to rule your own life. Abandon yourself to do His will. Early Christians were known by their confession, "Jesus is Lord."

Now pray this prayer by faith and the gift of salvation will be yours:

> Heavenly Father, I come to You in Jesus' name. I cannot save myself. Only You can save me. I confess my sins. Forgive me by Your grace. I accept Your forgiveness for all my sins. I receive Jesus now as my Lord and Savior. I give You my life in full surrender to Your will.
>
> I put my faith in Christ alone to save me. I receive the free gift of eternal life now.
>
> I believe Your promise. I am a new person. My sins are gone. I have eternal life. Jesus is Lord of my life from this moment on. I will serve Him with all my heart.
>
> In Jesus' name. Amen.

Welcome to the family of God! Now, prepare for an exciting life as you grow spiritually in your relationship to Christ. When doubt or discouragement comes, shake it off; and remember that God will finish the work He has started in you.

I leave you with this promise: "Being confident of this, that he who began a good work in you will carry it on to completion until the day of Christ Jesus" (Philippians 1:6).

What Is a Christian?

We tend to get religion and nationality confused. We speak of Christian, Muslim or Buddhist nations. A few years ago, my wife, Barbie, and I led a tour group to Turkey. In Istanbul, we made the mistake of getting into a taxi with a driver who spoke very little English, and we spoke absolutely no Turkish. We wanted him to take us to a restaurant about 10 minutes away to meet a group of friends for lunch.

Talk about a communications breakdown! We ended up taking an unplanned scenic tour of Istanbul, which lasted over an hour and cost me $50! But I learned an important lesson—one in addition to the lesson of never getting into a Turkish cab again! I learned that people think of religion in terms of nationality.

We struck up the best conversation we could, considering our limited knowledge of each other's language. (When you spend nearly an hour together in a cab, it's amazing how much you can learn of another language.)

179

After talking about our families, how many children we had and so forth, he asked me what I did for a living. This took a while to explain. First Barbie said, "He's a doctor." I knew that he wouldn't understand that since my doctorate is in theology not medicine. So she tried, "Minister." That didn't register either. She then tried, "Preacher." No response. Finally, I made the sign of the cross with my fingers and said, "Christian." He smiled and nodded his head indicating that he was familiar with the word *Christian*.

So, I asked him, "Are you a Christian?"

He replied, "No. Muslim." Then he added, "Europeans, Americans—Christians." He thought of religion in terms of nationality.

Research indicates that the vast majority of Americans identify their religious affiliation as Christian. So, what is a Christian?

Some people view Christianity as merely a *religion* consisting of beliefs, worship and a code of conduct. Others define it in terms of *rituals* with services, sacraments, sacred days and symbols. Some view it as a system of *regulations* consisting of laws, rules and moral standards; a long list of do's and don'ts. Still others see the Christian life as *reorientation* characterized by self-improvement, positive thinking and getting in touch with one's spirituality.

Religion or Relationship?

The word *Christian* actually comes from two words: *Christ* and *man*. Christ living in a man; a man living in Christ. A Christian, then, is an individual who has a

180

personal relationship with Jesus Christ—a relationship that influences every aspect of life. A Roman official, in second century A.D., wrote an intriguing letter describing Christians:

> Christians are not differentiated from other people by country, language, or customs; you see, they do not live in cities of their own, or speak some strange dialect . . . They live in both Greek and foreign cities, wherever chance has put them.

> They follow local customs in clothing, food, and the other aspects of life. But at the same time, they demonstrate to us the unusual form of their own citizenship. They live in their own native lands, but as aliens. . . . Every foreign country is to them as their native country, and every native land as a foreign country. They marry and have children just like everyone else, but they do not kill unwanted babies. They offer a shared table, but not a shared bed. They are passing their days on earth, but are citizens of heaven. They obey the appointed laws and go beyond the law in their own lives.

> They love everyone, but are persecuted by all. They are put to death and gain life. They are poor yet make many rich. They are dishonored and yet gain glory through dishonor. Their names are blackened and yet they are cleared. They are mocked and bless in return. They are treated outrageously and behave respectfully to others. When they do good they are punished as evildoers; when punished, they rejoice as if being given new life.

Sometimes, Christians don't act very Christian. A minister's 5-year-old son asked him, "Dad, what is a Christian?"

His father explained that Christians believe in Christ, read the Bible, pray, love others, do what is right, control their tempers, never speak a harsh word, and are always kind. Puzzled by the answer, the boy asked, "Dad, have I ever seen a Christian?" When we examine ourselves, and the way we act on occasion, we too are prone to ask, "Have I ever seen a Christian?"

But the Christian life isn't perfection; it's progression. I once read, "The conversion of a soul is the miracle of a moment, the manufacture of a saint is the task of a lifetime."

People do not become Christians in mass as when Emperor Constantine baptized the entire Roman army as Christians. Later, Emperor Theodosius I declared Christianity to be the state religion of Rome. The Gospel of John records 27 personal conversations between Jesus and an individual. Salvation is personal.

Christianity is not a matter of family history, cultural identity or nationality. A person becomes a Christian when he or she believes in Jesus as Lord and Savior. "Believe in the Lord Jesus, and you will be saved—you and your household" (Acts 16:31).

Jesus said, "No one can see the kingdom of God unless he is born again" (John 3:3). To be "born again" or "born from above" is to experience a spiritual transformation. The moment we confess our sins to God and believe in Jesus Christ as Lord, we are born again.

If I could summarize the work of God in our lives in one word, it would be *transformation*. To transform is to change the character, nature, condition or form of something. We are changed from death to life, from sin to righteousness and from eternal condemnation to eternal life. Colossians 1:13 says, "For he has rescued us from the dominion of darkness and brought us into the kingdom of the Son he loves."

To be a Christian is not a self-effort program whereby we attempt to turn over a new leaf and seek to live morally pure lives. I've listened to people say, "I am going to start trying to be a Christian." That's impossible! A person becomes a Christian by trusting Jesus. It is in trusting, not trying, that we are saved. John writes, "Yet to all who received [Jesus], to those who believed in his name, he gave the right to become children of God—children born not of natural descent, nor of human decision or a husband's will, but born of God" (John 1:12, 13). The apostle Paul describes it this way:

> That if you confess with your mouth, "Jesus is Lord," and believe in your heart that God raised him from the dead, you will be saved. For it is with your heart that you believe and are justified, and it is with your mouth that you confess and are saved. For, "Everyone who calls on the name of the Lord will be saved" (Romans 10:9, 10, 13).

LEARNING THE LANGUAGE

Every field of study—mathematics, science, psychology, sociology, theology—has its own language. The mastery of any field of study requires the student to learn the language of that academic discipline. When we read the Bible, we encounter the language of faith. Powerful, life-changing words appear throughout its pages that explain what it means to be a Christian.

The word *salvation* means "deliverance, wholeness and soundness." In Christ, we are delivered and set free from the guilt and control of sin. We are made whole and complete. Iraeneus said, "The glory of God is a human being who is fully alive."

The good news of Jesus is that the gospel "is the power of God for the salvation of everyone who believes" (see Romans 1:16). "For it is by grace you have been saved, through faith—and this is not from yourselves, it is the gift of God" (Ephesians 2:8). We are saved by grace through faith. Grace means that salvation is a free gift. Faith means that we receive the gift of salvation by trusting in Christ, and in Him alone.

Contemporary author Max Lucado writes, "If there are a thousand steps between us and [God], but He will take all but one. But He will leave the final one for us. The choice is ours." That step is the bold step of faith.

Justification is basically a judicial term that means "to pardon from guilt and to declare a person righteous." As incredible as it seems, Jesus bore our sins on the cross and paid the penalty for them. God pardons us of our sins when we trust Him and credits to our account the righteousness of Christ.

When God sees us, He doesn't see our sins. He sees us dressed in the garments of the righteousness of Christ. "God made him who had no sin to be sin for us, so that in him we might become the righteousness of God" (2 Corinthians 5:21). That's the "great exchange"—our sin for His righteousness.

Believers are made holy and set apart for the glory of God. Holiness carries the idea of being special, unique and different. The word *saint* comes from the word "sanctify." If you are like me, you're not comfortable calling yourself a saint. Believe it or not, as a Christian you are, as far as God is concerned, a saint. Paul addressed the Corinthians as "saints in Christ Jesus," even though they had a host of spiritual problems (see 2 Corinthians 1:1). Sainthood is a gift of grace, not the result of good deeds.

You have been set apart for His sacred use. Jesus suffered on the cross "to make the people holy through his own blood" (Hebrews 13:12). The Temple of God was holy because it was different from other buildings. The priests were holy because they were different from other men. The Sabbath is holy because it is different from other days. The tithe is holy because it is different from other money. The Bible is holy because it is different from other books. The church is holy because it is different from other organizations.

Here's a humorous look at holiness. Two brothers are in the Mafia. One dies, so his brother goes to a priest who knew the reputation of the two brothers and requests a Christian burial. The man promised the church a substantial financial gift if the priest would only use the word *saint* in the eulogy for his brother.

The priest agrees to preach the funeral. He struggles to think of a way to incorporate the word *saint* in his remarks. During the eulogy the priest tells the congregation, "As you all know, the man before us today was the worst, low-down, no-good, scoundrel who trafficked in a life of crime. But compared to his brother, he was a saint!"

185

Sin puts us at enmity with God. Sin is a barrier, which separates us from His presence. When we receive God's forgiveness the barrier is removed and we are at peace with Him. The relationship severed by sin is mended by grace.

One of my favorite passages is Romans 5:1, 2: "Therefore, since we have been justified through faith, we have peace with God through our Lord Jesus Christ, through whom we have gained access by faith into this grace in which we now stand." We can approach God with freedom and confidence because we are at peace with Him.

Redemption is an old word, which means to purchase something back that has been lost. It also means to set free that which has been held captive. In ancient times the word was used to describe purchasing back property that had been lost. It also was used in reference to buying a slave.

These are the two sides of the coin of redemption— ransom and deliverance. Jesus said, "The Son of Man [came] . . . to give his life as a ransom for many" (Mark 10:45). Christ has purchased us by His blood out of the slavery of sin and has given us a certificate of freedom. We serve Him out of love not fear; out of choice not coercion. Listen to the song of the redeemed: "You are worthy . . . because you were slain, and with your blood you purchased men for God from every tribe and language and people and nation" (Revelation 5:9).

From Revelation To Revolution

Christianity begins as a revelation of Christ, but leads to a revolution—first, of the self, then, of society. The world is changed one heart at a time. "Therefore, if anyone is in Christ, he is a new creation; the old has gone, the new has come!" (2 Corinthians 5:17). When Christ enters the human heart a revolution occurs. "Follow me," Jesus said in Matthew 4:19, "and I will make you." Let those words sink deep in your heart—*I will make you.* He promises to mold our lives into His own likeness as we follow Him. Following Jesus means to maintain a close relationship of trust and obedience.

Christians are Christ-made, not self-made. The whole sphere of a person's life is revolutionized by the influence of Christ. Young people wear jewelry with the initials, *WWJD?* The question, *What would Jesus do?* is a revolutionary question that impacts every aspect of one's life.

Toward the end of the 19th century, Swedish chemist Alfred Nobel awoke one morning to read his own obituary in the local newspaper: "Alfred Nobel, the inventor of dynamite, who died yesterday, devised a way for more people to be killed in a war than ever before, and he died a very rich man."

Actually, it was Alfred's brother who had died; a reporter had botched the obituary. The account had a profound effect on Alfred Nobel. He decided that he wanted to be known for something other than inventing the means for killing people in war, and for amassing great wealth in the process.

So he initiated the Nobel Peace Prize, the award for those who foster peace. He said, "Every man ought to have the chance to correct his epitaph in midstream and write a new one." Jesus gives us the opportunity to change the direction of our lives as we learn to follow Him.

Christianity is a revolution of life. The American Red Cross was gathering supplies, medicine, clothing and food for the suffering people of Biafra. Inside one of the boxes that showed up at the collecting depot one day was a letter which read: "We have recently been converted to Christ and because of our conversion we want to try to help. We won't ever need these again. Can you use them for something worthwhile?"

Inside the boxes were Ku Klux Klan sheets. The sheets were cut into strips and eventually used to bandage the wounds of the suffering in Africa. That's a revolution of the human heart. Hatred was turned to love.

A letter written by Cyprian, third century bishop of Carthage, to his friend, Donatus, captures the revolution of Christianity:

> It's a bad world, Donatus, an incredibly bad world. But I have discovered in the midst of it, a quiet and good people who have learned the secret of life. They have found a joy and wisdom which is a thousand times better than any pleasures of our sinful life. They are despised and persecuted, but they care not. They have overcome the world. These people, Donatus, are Christians—and I am one of them.

Faith and Repentance

A person becomes a Christian, a follower of Christ, through faith and repentance. That's what God requires. When Peter preached on the day of Pentecost, the people asked, "What shall we do?" Peter replied, "Repent and be baptized . . . in the name of Jesus Christ for the forgiveness of your sins. And you will receive the gift of the Holy Spirit" (Acts 2:37, 38).

The watchwords of Christianity are *by faith*! "We live by faith, not by sight" (2 Corinthians 5:7). Here are the ABCs of faith:

First, faith *acknowledges* Jesus as Lord. Faith begins when you intellectually believe that Jesus is who He claimed to be—the Son of God, the Messiah and Lord of all. "If you confess with your mouth, 'Jesus is Lord,' and believe in your heart that God raised him from the dead, you will be saved" (Romans 10:9).

Faith is not blind; it sees clearly. Christianity is not only a matter of the heart; it's also a matter of the mind. We have to think right to live right. Those who say, "It doesn't matter what you believe as long as you believe something, and you're sincere in your beliefs," couldn't be more wrong.

Faith is based on the historical and factual evidence of Jesus Christ, the risen Lord. A person has to come to terms with the claims of Jesus as the Son of God, the Messiah and Lord of all. Faith, then, begins with an understanding that Jesus is the Son of God.

C.S. Lewis, the noted Oxford scholar, became a Christian through an intellectual investigation of the claims of Jesus. After his research, he concluded that Jesus either had to be a liar of epidemic proportions, a lunatic running around claiming to be the Messiah, or the Lord of all. Lewis put his faith in Jesus Christ as Lord and became one of the 20th century's most influential Christians, writing such classics as *The Screwtape Letters* and *Mere Christianity.*

Second, faith *believes* in Jesus as Savior. Emotionally, we trust Him to save us from our sins and to give us the gift of eternal life. "For it is with your heart that you believe and are justified (that means "declared righteous before God, pardoned of all sins"), and it is with your mouth that you confess and are saved. As the Scripture says, 'Everyone who trusts in him will never be put to shame'" (Romans 10:10, 11, parenthesis added).

Trust is as emotional as it is intellectual. We experience peace when we trust Christ to keep us through every situation of life.

Third, faith *commits* everything to Christ in full devotion. First the mind, then the emotions and finally, the human will. The fruit of faith is obedience to the will of Christ. Jesus said, "If you love me, you will obey what I command" (John 14:15).

Faith begins with a revelation of Christ but results in a revolution as we seek to imitate Christ in every area of life. "This is how we know we are in him: Whoever claims to live in him must walk as Jesus did" (1 John 2:5, 6).

The Apostle's Creed, written around A.D. 700, was provided to give believers in every generation the basics of faith. Take time to read it aloud.

I believe in God the Father Almighty, maker of heaven and earth. And in Jesus Christ His only Son, our Lord; who was conceived by the Holy Spirit, born of the Virgin Mary, suffered unto Pontius Pilate, was crucified, dead and buried; He descended into Hades; the third day He rose again from the dead; He ascended into heaven, and sits on the right hand of God, the Father Almighty; from whence He shall come to judge the quick and the dead. I believe in the Holy Spirit, the holy Christian church, the communion of saints, the forgiveness of sins, the resurrection of the body, and the life everlasting. Amen.

Coupled with faith is repentance. Repentance is not a negative word. In fact, it's the first word of the gospel. Jesus preached, "Repent, for the kingdom of heaven is near" (Matthew 4:17). The first of the 95 theses Martin Luther nailed to the door of the Church of Wittenberg, read, "When our Lord and Master Jesus Christ said 'Repent,' he willed the entire life of believers to be one of repentance."

In 1842, the first bathtub was denounced as a "luxurious and democratic vanity." Boston made it unlawful to bathe, except on a physician's order. In 1843, Philadelphia made bathing illegal between November 1 and March 15. Sounds ludicrous, doesn't it? No more ludicrous as those who deny the reality of sin and the need of a spiritual bath in the waters of divine grace.

Our deepest spiritual need is to be cleansed from sin, guilt and failure. Cleansing comes to those who honestly confess their sins. In his book *Born Again*, Chuck Colson talks about his experiences during Watergate. He describes one of President Nixon's problems as being unable or unwilling to admit he was wrong about anything. Even when Nixon had a cold with all the obvious symptoms, he wouldn't admit it.

Americans were deeply troubled when former President Bill Clinton lied on national television to his own staff and to the American people about his affair with a White House intern. Again, it was a case of a person's inability to say, "I was wrong. I'm sorry."

When you hear the word *repentance,* what comes to your mind? Do you picture Jonah, fresh out of the belly of a whale, walking into Nineveh covered with seaweed, smelling like a fish, declaring to the Ninevites, *Repent?*

Or John the Baptist in the Judean wilderness, dressed in camel's hair, with eyes of fire confronting everyone from religious aristocrats to the common man with the message, *Repent*! Or maybe a fanatic on the street corner of a metropolitan city carrying a sign reading, *Repent*!

Repentance means a change of mind and direction of life. The word *repent* comes from two Greek words meaning, "to perceive afterwards" (*meta* means "after," implying change; and *noeo*, means "to perceive," from *nous*, the mind or seat of moral reflection). The good news of Jesus causes one to change his mind and direction in life. The word *repentance* is always used in Scripture of changing one's mind for the better. When we repent we turn away from sin and turn toward God. Stop, turn around and go in the opposite direction. That's repentance.

Jesus' parable of the prodigal son provides a clear picture of repentance (see Luke 15:11-24). A rebellious son took his inheritance and left home. He turned his back on his father and traveled to a far, distant country. He eventually went bankrupt after spending all his money on licentious living. He got a humble job feeding pigs and eating the corns husks the pigs left behind.

When he hit rock bottom, he came to his senses. He had a change of mind. Then, he said to himself, "I will set out and go back to my father" (v. 18). That's a change of purpose. Finally, he made the journey home, which describes a change of direction. Instead of moving away from his father, he went back to him. His change of direction eventually took him back home. So it is with us. Repentance means we stop running from God, turn around and run toward Him. And He always welcomes us with open arms.

Lost and Found

I think that if we were to ask Jesus, "What is a Christian?" He would answer, "A Christian is a person who was once lost but is now found." Jesus came into the world to "seek and to save what was lost" (Luke 19:10).

A prominent Jewish rabbi admits that this is the one new thing Jesus taught about God—that God searched for humanity. Actually, it is taught in Genesis. The Bible begins with a portrait of the God who searches for those who are lost. When Adam and Eve sinned in Eden, God came looking for them. "Where are you?" He asked (Genesis 3:9). God always seeks us out when we are lost. The Christian's testimony is not, "I found the Lord," but rather, "The Lord found me!" After all, God has never been lost.

One summer Barbie, the children and I were on vacation in Florida. Barbie left the beach to go back to the room. Our son, David Paul, was swimming in the ocean. My daughter Charlsi (who was 4 at the time) and I were building a sand castle. I was busy at work on our masterpiece when suddenly I realized she was gone. Panic gripped me. I ran to the room and got Barbie. She and I, along with David Paul, ran madly down the beach in opposite directions looking for her. We screamed out her name, in tones mixed with fear and hope, searching desperately.

About 10 minutes later (which seemed like eternity) a police car drove up on the beach. The police officer got out of the car holding our little girl. What a moment of reunion. We held her tightly and said a prayer of thanks to God.

She had gone down to the water's edge to get some shells for our castle. She got confused and started wandering down the beach looking for me. A lady saw that she looked lost and called the beach patrol.

193

There is no experience more frightening than being lost. The difference between my daughter and many people is that she knew she was lost. Once you know you're lost, you are ready for Christ to find you.

Perfection or Progression?

Have you seen this bumper sticker? *Be patient with me—God's not through with me yet!* When commenting on spiritual growth, C. S. Lewis remarked, "You can't just be a good egg forever." Growth is fundamental to life. We either grow or we die. We either develop or we deteriorate. We either progress or we regress.

Jesus' use of the words "born again" implies that a growth process follows conversion. Just as a newborn baby develops, so does a new Christian. The apostle Peter wrote in his Epistle, "Like newborn babies, crave pure spiritual milk, so that by it you may grow up in your salvation" (1 Peter 2:2).

The Christian life is a lifelong journey in which God gradually conforms us to the image of Christ. John Bunyan, in his classic *Pilgrim's Progress,* captures the real meaning of the Christian life as a journey of faith. Think of spiritual growth as a direction, not a destination.

The essential point is not to arrive at a state of perfection, but to enjoy the journey. "And we, who with unveiled faces all reflect the Lord's glory, are being transformed into his likeness with *ever-increasing glory*, which comes from the Lord, who is the Spirit" (2 Corinthians 3:18, emphasis added). I want to underscore the words "ever-increasing glory."

You will not always see your progress, but God is at work in you. Growth takes time. Changes in character, temperament and behavior take place gradually. God even uses our failures. Sometimes the Christian life is *three steps forward and two steps back!* But at least you are one step ahead of where you were!

Every honest Christian can say, *I'm not the person I want to be, but praise God, I'm not the person I used to be!*

A court painter once painted a portrait of Oliver Cromwell, who was afflicted with warts on his face. Thinking he would please the great man, the painter omitted the warts. When Cromwell saw the painting, he said, "Take it away! Paint me warts and all!"

The longer we live the Christian life, the more grateful we become for the grace of God. We move from self-sufficiency to Christ-sufficiency. Such is the nature of true humility. This maturity in humility is clearly seen in the writings of the apostle Paul.

- In the first letter he wrote, he introduces himself as "Paul, an apostle" (Galatians 1:1).

- Later, at the height of his ministry, he writes, "I am the least of the apostles" (1 Corinthians 15:9).

- Toward the end of his ministry he writes, I "am the less than the least of all the saints" (Ephesians 3:8, *NKJV*). A saint was an ordinary member of the church.

- In one his last letters, written shortly before his execution by Nero, he admits he is the chief of sinners (see 1 Timothy 1:15).

195

He wasn't suffering from low self-esteem. He was coming to terms with the amazing grace of God. His testimony was simple: "By the grace of God I am what I am" (1 Corinthians 15:10). As the years passed, he became more deeply aware of his own inadequacy, yet more assured of the all-sufficiency of Christ. On one hand, he says he has nothing. Yet, he claims, "I can do everything through him who gives me strength" (Philippians 4:13).

It has been said that the gate of heaven is so low that no one can enter it except upon his knees.

While the word *Christian* appears only three times in the New Testament, the word *disciple* is used nearly 300 times. A disciple is a learner, a follower and an imitator of Jesus. Basically, a disciple is a student. Jesus said, "Take my yoke upon you and learn from me" (Matthew 11:29).

The primary work of the Holy Spirit, through every event and experience of life, is to make us more like Jesus. "We know that in all things God works for the good of those who love him, who have been called according to his purpose. For those God foreknew he also predestined *to be conformed to the likeness of his Son*" (Romans 8:28, 29, emphasis added).

How do we grow spiritually? "So then, just as you received Christ Jesus as Lord, continue to live in him, rooted and built up in him, strengthened in the faith as you were taught, and overflowing with thankfulness" (Colossians 2:6, 7).

Spiritual growth is summed up in three action words: *Rooted, strengthened, overflowing.*

Rooted

First, we need to develop deep spiritual roots. The word *rooted* is past tense describing a definite act in the past, namely, our salvation. We are once and for all rooted in Christ when we believe in Him. The phrase *built up* is present tense describing the continual action of developing a spiritual foundation.

We are built up "in Him." Christ is the soil in which we are planted. We aren't called to follow an idea, a system or a religion. We are called to follow Him, to know Him and to pledge our loyalty to Him.

Roots provide nourishment and stability. Think about the Chinese bamboo tree. When planted, the seed remains in the soil for five years with no signs of growth. Then, in the 5th year it grows 80 feet, all because of its root system.

The Japanese art of *bonsai*, or miniaturizing living trees, is done, first of all, by cutting off the taproot. The tree then obtains nourishment only through smaller surface roots and its growth is greatly reduced. The same process can occur with us. Without deep roots nourished by the Word of God and the fellowship of other believers, we live only through surface roots, which in turn results in stunted spiritual growth. Spiritual growth occurs through relationships with other believers.

John Donne's statement, "No man is an island entire of itself," is certainly true of the Christian life. Every Christian needs three relationships: A mentor like Paul, an encourager like Barnabas and a disciple like Timothy.

Strengthened

Second, Paul says to be *strengthened in the faith.* A strong faith is needed to handle life's pressures, adversities and temptations. Faith is strengthened by reading and hearing the Word of God. "Faith comes from hearing the message, and the message is heard through the word of Christ" (Romans 10:17).

Faith also grows stronger when it is put to use. A strong faith is an active faith. When you experience the promises of God, your faith becomes unshakable.

A couple in my congregation met me after a worship service. "We want to share our miracle with you," they said with big smiles on their faces. They showed me their beautiful, newborn baby girl. Then they handed me a note with Psalm 113:9 written on it: "He settles the barren woman in her home as a happy mother of children. Praise the Lord."

They told me that God had given them that verse during our New Year's Eve service. The woman had been unable to conceive a child. But they claimed the promise by faith. Ten months later they gave birth to their first child, a little girl. Faith had become a reality in their lives.

Overflowing

The third action word Paul uses to describe spiritual growth is *overflowing.* Israel has two main bodies of water—the Sea of Galilee in the north and the Dead Sea in the south. Three streams of water flow from the mountains in the north to form the fountainhead of the Jordan River. The Jordan River flows into the Sea of Galilee and exits the sea on the south where it flows through the land of Israel until finally pouring out into the Dead Sea.

For centuries, rabbis have used the example of these two bodies of water to illustrate two types of people. Some are like the Sea of Galilee. Its fresh waters are filled with fish and its banks are surrounded by lush, fertile land. The Sea has three inlets and an outlet that allows water to pass through. The continual inflow and outflow of its waters keep it fresh.

Others, however, are like the Dead Sea. It has an inlet from the Jordan River but no outlet. Consequently, it has a 33 percent salt and mineral content, making its waters thick and oily. Every year more and more of the Dead Sea disappears through evaporation. The land around the Dead Sea is a desert. Its salty waters prohibit life and growth.

What kind of Christian are you? Are you a Sea of Galilee Christian who receives the abundance of God's blessings and then joyfully shares what God has given you with others? Or, are you a Dead Sea Christian, always receiving but never giving?

Joy comes when we experience the cycle of grace. "Freely you have received, freely give" (Matthew 10:8). Paul says we are to overflow with thankfulness (see Colossians 2:7). The word *overflow* means to spill over, the way a river swells during a flood and overflows its banks. It means "superabundance." Pour out to others as God pours into you, and your life will always overflow with joy. Keep the cycle of grace always moving in your life.

While we are not saved *by* good works, we are saved *for* good works. Jesus said, "Let your light shine before men, that they may see your good deeds and praise your Father in heaven" (Matthew 5:16). We need to keep the emphasis on *good* works, not just works. There is the problem of slipping back into the dead works of the old life we lived before we knew Christ. We also run the danger of prideful works like the Pharisees who practiced their religion only to be praised by men.

The word *good* describes that which is good in its character, morally honorable and pleasing to God, as well as, that which benefits others. Paul reminds us that we are "God's workmanship, created in Christ Jesus to do good works, which God prepared in advance for us to do" (Ephesians 2:10). The word *workmanship* can also be translated as *masterpiece.* Just as people go to famous art galleries to view great works of art, God wants His grace to be displayed in our lives so people can see Christ in us.

Pour out as God Pours in

The principle of overflowing was brought home to me in an unforgettable way in 1994 when I attended the National Day of Prayer Breakfast in Washington, D.C. Mother Teresa was the keynote speaker. She spoke with such deep conviction on behalf of those suffering around the world.

Her words poured onto our hearts like hot lava from the throne of God. She had truly learned what it means to share in the sufferings of Christ. She was a Christian who was moved with compassion. She shared an account of a man who came to her headquarters one night pleading for food on behalf of a starving family:

> I had the most extraordinary experience of love of neighbor with a Hindu family. A gentleman came to our house and said: "Mother Teresa, there is a family who has not eaten for so long. Do something." So I took some rice and

went there immediately. And I saw the children—their eyes shining with hunger. I don't know if you have ever seen hunger. But I have seen it often. And the mother of the family took the rice I gave her and went out. When she came back, I asked her: "Where did you go? What did you do?" And she gave me a very simple answer: "They are hungry also." What struck me was that she knew. And who are they? A Muslim family—and she knew. I didn't bring any more rice that evening because I wanted them, Hindus and Muslims, to enjoy the joy of sharing.

The apostle James tells us, "faith without deeds is dead" (James 2:26). He also challenges the validity of faith if there are no works of love.

What good is it, my brothers, if a man claims to have faith but has no deeds? Can such faith save him? Suppose a brother or sister is without clothes and daily food. If one of you says to him, "Go, I wish you well; keep warm and well fed," but does nothing about his physical needs, what good is it? In the same way, faith by itself, if it is not accompanied by action, is dead (James 2:14-17).

The word *religion* is used only once in the New Testament and it is in reference to good works. "Religion that God our Father accepts as pure and faultless is this: to look after orphans and widows in their distress and to keep oneself from being polluted by the world" (James 1:27).

All God's children are gifted children. We all have three gifts to give back as we keep the cycle of grace moving in our lives—time, talent and treasure. So, devote your time to serving Christ. Use your talents and gifts for His glory by serving others. And give financially as an act of worship to God and to support the gospel. God gives us time, talents and treasure and expects us to make an investment in the kingdom.

Erma Bombeck said, "When I stand before God at the end of my life, I would hope that I would not have a single bit of talent left but could say, 'I used everything you gave me.'"

The Sunday was stormy and many people remained home instead of coming to church. One teacher decided, however, to hold a service in a little Wesleyan Chapel in Colchester, England. One young man accepted Christ at the meeting. His name was Charles Spurgeon, and he became the most influential preacher in London during the late 1800s. His sermons still inspire untold numbers of believers.

Serve your way to joy. Don't be like the Dead Sea, always receiving and never giving. You will only become ingrown, stagnant and unproductive. Be like the Sea of Galilee, receiving the mighty inflow of God's blessings and then pour those blessings out to others. Your life will be joyful, enriched and productive.

"Preach always—and if necessary, use words" (Francis of Assisi).

The Acid Test
Love is the measure of the Christian life.

We know and rely on the love God has for us. God is love. Whoever lives in love lives in God, and God in him . . . There is no fear in love. But perfect love drives out fear, because fear has to do with punishment. The one who fears is not made perfect in love. We love because he first loved us (1 John 4:16, 18, 19).

The perfect love of God drives out the fears of failure, rejection, judgment, insecurity and even death. The love of God is a healing ointment for the wounds of the soul and the fears of the mind.

Love sums up the Christian life. We trust Christ to save us because we have come to know and experience His love. Only when we know the love of God are we free to love others. The royal law, "Love your neighbor as yourself," answers the question, How should a Christian live? Paul tells us, "The entire law is summed up in a single command, 'Love your neighbor as yourself'" (Galatians 5:14). The only command Jesus gave us is the command to love. "A new command I give you: Love one another. As I have loved you, so you must love one another" (John 13:34).

It is said that Mao Tse Tung came to America seeking a western education and exposure to Christianity. When he faced discrimination, he left disillusioned and turned to Marxism. The rest is history.

Loveless Christianity is powerless to change the world. "By this," said Jesus, "all men will know that you are my disciples, if you love one another" (v. 35). Jesus will not allow us the luxury of compartmentalizing our lives into spiritual and natural spheres. We cannot talk about spiritual life apart from all the other aspects of life.

A teacher of Jewish law asked Jesus, "Which is the greatest commandment in the Law?" He replied, "Love the Lord your God with all your heart and with all your soul and with all your mind." But then quickly added, "And the second is like it: 'Love your neighbor as yourself'" (see Matthew 22:35-39).

Jesus will not permit us to talk about our relationship with God apart from our relationships with others. The measure of our love for others is the measure of our love for God. "Whoever loves God must also love his brother" (1 John 4:21).

What kind of love is Christian love? Love is *selfless*— Christ pleased not Himself. Love *serves*—Christ came not to be served but to serve and to give His life for all. Love *sacrifices*—Christ gave himself up as a fragrant offering and sacrifice to God for our sins. To be a Christian is not only to believe in Christ, it is to love with the love of Christ.

God Finishes What He Starts

Here's some great news: *God promises to complete the work He started in you!* "Being confident of this, that he who began a good work in you will carry it on to completion until the day of Christ Jesus" (Philippians 1:6).

You will make many mistakes and fail to reach many goals as a Christian. But take heart, "We all stumble in many ways," says the apostle James (3:2). When you fall, confess your sins to God, then get back up and keep on going on your Christian journey. John tells us, "If we confess our sins, he is faithful and just and will forgive us our sins and purify us from all unrighteousness" (1 John 1:9).

What Is a Christian?

You may also go through times when you lose your enthusiasm. You may even feel as though you're not really saved. We all are subject to changing emotions. But we live by faith, not by feelings. Never measure your relationship to God by your feelings. God is faithful regardless of your feelings. He promises, "Never will I leave you; never will I forsake you" (Hebrews 13:5).

When we fail, we feel like hypocrites. Just because you fail doesn't make you a hypocrite. The word *hypocrite* comes from Greek drama and means an actor on a stage. In a drama, actors play the part of characters. Since the actor is "acting," he or she is a hypocrite. The word came to mean one who pretends to be something he's not. Hypocrites intentionally deceive others to take advantage of them.

When a Christian sins, or struggles with a spiritual issue in his life, or fails to be a good witness for Christ, he needs to confess and repent of his sins. But his imperfection does not make him a hypocrite. You can be confident of God's love. Paul the apostle asks, "Who shall separate us from the love of Christ? Shall trouble or hardship or persecution or famine or nakedness or danger or sword?" (Romans 8:35).

He then gives a resounding response:

No, in all these things we are more than conquerors through him who loved us. For I am convinced that neither death nor life, neither angels nor demons, neither the present nor the future, nor any powers, neither height nor depth, nor anything else in all creation, will be able to separate us from the love of God that is in Christ Jesus our Lord (vv. 37-39).

205

Someone asked me recently, "What do you believe about eternal security?" I replied, "I only plan on being saved once."

God promises security if we trust in Him. Your eternal salvation is based on God's grace and power to keep you, not the level of your spiritual performance. Here is one of the most reassuring promises in the Bible: "To him who is able to keep you from falling and to present you before his glorious presence without fault and with great joy" (Jude 24). We are saved by grace and kept by grace. God is able to keep us for all eternity as we trust in Him.

There are two truths you need to know about God's love. First, you cannot do anything good to get God to love you more. Second, you cannot do anything bad to get God to love you less. Now, I'm not advocating irresponsibility. Actions certainly carry consequences. Besides, when we know that God loves us, we are motivated to obey Him. My point is, God's love is unconditional—no strings attached. Our love is conditional. We love *if.* . . . We love *because of.* . . . But God loves *in spite of* !

I have often pondered the difference between Christians who are joyful, positive and free versus those who are negative, legalistic and uptight. I am convinced it all boils down to love. As long as we fear God, in an unhealthy sense, and try to earn God's love by religious works, we will lack joy. But when we truly believe that God loves us, we will experience His joy.

I was speaking at a rally for a friend who is an evangelist. During the evening, he recognized several ministers who were present. One couple in particular, shared with us their testimony of God's grace. The man had been in prison for robbery. He was a crack addict and stole to support his habit. He became depressed in prison and decided to commit suicide. One day he made up his mind to hang himself that very night by using the bed sheet.

But coincidentally or divinely, during the day a parole officer came to see him. Surprisingly, she was not even assigned to his case.

"The Lord has sent me to give you a message from Him," she said confidently. "He wants you to know that He has a plan and purpose for your life." She went on to share God's plan of salvation with him.

That night, instead of ending his life, he began a new one. He knelt by his bed in the cell, and asked Christ to come into his life to save him. After his release, he started going back to the prison to minister to the inmates. Later, he resigned his job to go full-time in prison ministry.

He and his wife now minister regularly in 14 jails and prisons in northeast Georgia. He has led hundreds of inmates to know Jesus Christ—all because a parole officer listened to the Holy Spirit and cared enough to give him the greatest gift of all, the gospel of Jesus Christ.

10

Can We Trust the Bible?

Т he Bible is the book that has changed the world. It has done more to improve living conditions for humanity than any book ever written. What is the secret of its mysterious power? Simply stated, the Bible is not the word of men—it is the Word of God!

The Bible has been translated into over 1,600 languages and dialects, representing 97 percent of the world's known languages. It remains the best-selling book of all times. According to George Gallup, one in three Americans believe the Bible is the literal or inspired Word of God.

Yet, today the Bible is under attack. Skeptics abound with new assaults. For example, a cover of *Time* read, "Is the Bible Fact or Fiction?"[1] Surprisingly, the article presented many new archaeological evidences validating the historical accuracy of many Biblical narratives. The Jesus Seminar, a group of skeptic scholars, presumes to know exactly which portions of the Gospels are the authentic words of Jesus and which parts are not.

When the Jesus Seminar convened, however, it consisted of only 40 participants, many of whom were not even Biblical scholars. Some participants, such as Paul Verhoeven, director of the films *Basic Instinct* and *Showgirls*, merely participated as interested observers. This handful of liberals hardly represents nearly 9,000 members of the Society of Biblical Literature and thousands of seminary students, scholars and preachers of the gospel.

How We Got the Bible

The apostle Peter says, "Holy men of God spoke as they were moved by the Holy Spirit" (2 Peter 1:21, *NKJV*). God is the author, the mind behind the Book; however, He inspired men to write it.

The Bible consists of 66 books, written over 1,500 years by nearly 40 different authors from diverse backgrounds. The Old Testament was originally written in Hebrew, with parts of Daniel in Aramaic. The New Testament was written in Greek.

Moses authored the Law, also called the Torah or the Pentateuch, meaning "five books." Genesis consists primarily of patriarchal history, recording the lives of Abraham, Isaac, Jacob and Joseph. Genesis is our roots, revealing where we came from and why we are here.

Exodus through Deuteronomy records the life of Moses, the Exodus of Israel from Egyptian slavery, the law of God given at Sinai, and the messages Moses delivered to the people of Israel shortly before they entered the Promised Land. The Pentateuch closes with the account the account of Moses' death and the succession of Joshua as Israel's new leader.

Moses started the Hebrew tradition of keeping written historical records for generations to come. Perhaps he learned the importance of having such written records from growing up in Pharaoh's palace. There he was exposed to the ancient Egyptian libraries of learning. From the time of Moses, the Hebrews maintained the custom of recording their history.

Joshua recorded the conquest of Canaan. Samuel authored Judges, Ruth and 1 and 2 Samuel. King David, along with his appointed musical priests and his son, Solomon, recorded the Psalms (including one authored by Moses— Psalm 90). King Solomon wrote most of the Wisdom Literature. The Israeli kings had scribes and prophets keep records. The prophets had personal secretaries to record their messages.

About 300 years before the time of Christ, the Old Testament was canonized as it appears today with its 39 books, although the arrangement of the books was some-what different. The Hebrew Bible contains only 22 books, but has the same content as the 39 books of the Old Testament.

The apostles of Jesus recorded and preserved the Gospels and the apostolic letters of the New Testament. The Canon was completed around A.D. 400, validating the apostolic authority of the current 27 books that comprise the New Testament. The basic test for which books were included in the Canon was the test of apostolic authority. All 27 books are either the work of an apostle or a close associate of an apostle, such as Luke, Paul's companion, who authored the Gospel of Luke and the Acts of the Apostles, or John Mark, a close companion of the apostle Peter, who authored the Gospel of Mark.

Jerome translated the Scripture into the Latin Vulgate while living in the city of Bethlehem, around A.D. 400. Later, English versions were translated. John Wycliffe, church rector and Oxford scholar, produced the first completed English translation of the New Testament and parts of the Old Testament in 1382. His associates finished the work after his death in 1384.

William Tyndale translated the New Testament in 1525 and the Pentateuch in 1530. He was martyred in 1536. Other English translations include the King James Version (1611, also called the Authorized Version), the Revised Version (1885) and the *New International Version* (1978).

Is the Bible Ispired?

When Dwight L. Moody, an influential preacher of the 1800s, was asked why he believed the Bible is inspired, he replied, "Because it inspires me!" Most people believe that the Bible is inspired by God on some level. There are several different views of inspiration.[2]

The *natural inspiration or the intuition theory* suggests that divine inspiration is merely a superior insight on the part of the authors of Scripture into spiritual matters.

The *partial-inspiration theory* holds the position that God gave the authors the ability for reliable transmission and recording of the truth, which made them infallible in matters of faith but not in things of a nonreligious nature.

Others hold to the *theory that the thoughts, not the words,* are inspired. God suggested the thoughts or the content, while the actual words were those of the authors.

Some hold to the *theory that the Bible only contains the Word of God.* They believe that the Bible is a human book, which God can make His Word at the moment a person hears it.

The *dictation theory* suggests that the authors were pens in the hands of God. So no personal qualities of the authors are expressed in their writings.

All these theories fall short of the Bible's self-claim to plenary and verbal inspiration. The word *inspiration* means "God-breathed." Paul writes, "All Scripture is God-breathed" (2 Timothy 3:16, 17). When we think about the breath of God in Scripture, we think of the creation of Adam. "The Lord God formed the man from the dust of the ground and breathed into his nostrils the breath of life, and the man became a living being" (Genesis 2:7). In the Hebrew language of the Old Testament, the breath of God (*ruach*) is the same word used for the Spirit of God or for life itself.

Jesus said, "The words I have spoken to you are spirit and they are life" (John 6:63). Again, note the connection between spirit and life. The apostle Peter says, "Men spoke from God as they were carried along by the Holy Spirit" (2 Peter 1:21). The Holy Spirit carried the writers along, directing their thoughts, as the waters of the ocean carry a ship along. The writer of Hebrews claims, "The word of God is living and active" (4:12).

So the inspiration of Scripture means first, that God is the mind behind the Bible. Second, men wrote as direct-ed by the Holy Spirit. Third, God has preserved the accuracy of the writings (a fact verified by archaeology and the discovery of the Dead Sea Scrolls). Fourth, the Bible has a transforming impact on those who come in contact with it.

Several truths about inspiration are important:

1. *Inspiration is beyond explanation.* It reflects the miracle of God's grace and the work of the Holy Spirit.

2. *Inspiration is limited to the Biblical authors.* No other book is inspired like the Bible.

3. *Inspiration involved the guidance of the Holy Spirit as men wrote the material.*

4. *The Holy Spirit kept the authors from errors and omissions.*

5. *Inspiration is both plenary* (it includes everything contained in the Bible) *and verbal* (the actual words, not just the thoughts, are inspired).

How can we know that the Bible is inspired and accurate? It is the nature of God to reveal Himself. He has revealed Himself to us through creation, human conscience, life's circumstances, Jesus Christ and the church. It is logical to conclude that God would also reveal Himself through a written record. Furthermore, the Bible claims to be the Word of God—a claim which cannot be discounted. We cannot simply dismiss the Bible. Its inspiration and influence throughout history is undeniable.

The Claim of Christ

Jesus believed the Scripture to be inspired. He referred to the Old Testament as the Word of God (see Matthew 4:4). He taught from the Old Testament and brought great clarity to its message in a time when religion had distorted it.

"Do not think I have come to abolish the Law or the Prophets; I have not come to abolish them but to fulfill them" (5:17).

The Old Testament speaks of the Messiah. Jesus said, "You diligently study the Scriptures because you think that by them you possess eternal life. These are the Scriptures that testify about me, yet you refuse to come to me to have life" (John 5:39, 40).

Jesus elevated Scripture over the oral tradition of the rabbis. "You nullify the word of God for the sake of your tradition. . . . Isaiah was right when he prophesied about you . . . 'their teachings are but rules taught by men,'" He told the Pharisees (Matthew 15:6, 7, 9). In the Gospels, Jesus quotes directly from 24 Old Testament books, but never does He quote from apocryphal writings.

Over a period of 1,500 years, 40 authors representing 19 different occupations, wrote one simple message of God's love and His plan of salvation. The 66 books are marked by a spiritual, doctrinal, historical and prophetic unity that no one can deny. The authors were diverse, yet the Bible reads like the work of one single mind.

Jesus upheld the authority of Scripture. "The Scripture cannot be broken" (John 10:35). The Word of God is binding and carries the weight of the authority of God. We cannot dissect it and claim that certain passages are inspired but others are not. We must accept the entirety of Scripture as the inspired Word of God.

Spiritual error results from a lack of knowledge of the Scriptures. "You are in error," Jesus told the Sadducees, "because you do not know the Scriptures or the power of God" (Matthew 22:29).

Most remarkably, Jesus said, "I tell you the truth, until heaven and earth disappear, not the smallest letter, not the least stroke of a pen, will by any means disappear from the Law until everything is accomplished" (Matthew 5:18). The smallest letter in Greek is *iota*, which we use when we say, "It doesn't make one iota of difference." It is the nearest Greek equivalent to the smallest Hebrew letter, *yodh*. The Greek word for the phrase *least stroke of a pen*, means "horn" and was used to designate the slight embellishment or extension of certain letters of the Hebrew alphabet.

Jesus not only upheld the inspiration and authority of the Scripture, He claimed equal authority for His teachings, which have been preserved in the Gospels and the apostolic letters. "Heaven and earth will pass away," He said, "but my words will never pass away" (Matthew 24:35).

Fulfilled Prophecy

History confirms the prophetic accuracy of Scripture. The Old Testament contains some 300 prophecies about the coming of Jesus, the Messiah. Some of these include the following.

- Messiah would be born through the seed of Abraham (Genesis 12:3).

- He would be rejected (Psalm 22:1).

- His executioners would gamble for His clothing, which indeed happened at the cross (Psalm 22:18).

- Not a bone in His body would be broken (Psalm 34:20). The Roman soldiers came to break His legs as Christ hung on the cross, but did not because they found Him already dead.

The Old Testament foretells Jesus' resurrection (16:11) and His ascension into heaven (24:7-10). The prophet Isaiah said the Messiah would be born of a virgin, He would be called Immanuel and He would be a descendant of King David (7:14; 9:6, 7). The prophet also foretold that Messiah would be a light for the Gentiles . . . and today we see the worldwide spread of Christianity (9:1).

Isaiah also describes the Crucifixion in remarkable detail in 52:13—53:12, even noting the detail that Messiah would be buried with the rich (53:9). Jesus was buried in a tomb provided by a wealthy man, Joseph of Arimathea (John 19:38-42).

Micah prophesied that the Messiah would be born in Bethlehem, the town of King David (5:2). Zechariah envisioned the Messiah entering Jerusalem riding on a donkey and being hailed as king (9:9). He also prophesied that the Messiah would be betrayed for 30 pieces of silver (11:12), and that His body would be pierced (12:10).

The Old Testament also contains prophecies concerning nations. These prophecies are so clear and have been fulfilled with such accuracy that scholars today look to these prophecies to understand the times in which we live. The Old Testament foretold the restoration of Israel, which occurred in 1948 after the nation had been nonexistent for nearly 2,000 years (see Amos 9:11, 12; Ezekiel 37:1-11).

The prophet Ezekiel prophesied that the mighty Egyptian empire would become "the lowliest of kingdoms" (see 29:13-15). He gave the prophecy around 600 B.C. His

217

prophecy was fulfilled when Alexander the Great conquered Egypt in 332 B.C. Egypt has never regained its former glory.

Daniel foresaw the collapse of Babylon (539 B.C.), the rise of Medo-Persia, the conquests of Greece under Alexander the Great, and the division of the Greek empire into four smaller empires after Alexander's untimely death. He also predicted the rise of Rome (63 B.C.) and the Syrian invasion of Israel and Egypt under Antiochus Epiphanes IV, which took place between 168 and 165 B.C. He describes the coming of the Antichrist in the last days.

Ezekiel prophesied the demise of Tyre, the great Phoenician harbor city. In 590 B.C. he predicted the great city would one day be submerged under the sea. Alexander conquered it in 332 B.C. Today, you can go snorkeling over the ruins of ancient Tyre, which is submerged under the waters of the Mediterranean.

Nahum the prophet foretold the complete destruction of Nineveh, the capital of the Assyrian Empire, in 650 B.C. His prophecy was fulfilled in August 612 B.C., when the Medes and Persians conquered the city. Later, Alexander marched his troops over the remains of Nineveh in 330 B.C. and never even knew a city had existed there because the destruction by the Medes and Persians had been so complete.

Jesus predicted the complete overthrow of Jerusalem and the destruction of the Temple. "I tell you the truth, not one stone here will be left on another; every one will be thrown down" (Matthew 24:2). His sobering words came to pass in A.D. 70 when Titus and the Roman army conquered Jerusalem and destroyed the Temple.

The Bible also records prophecies about influential persons. In 712 B.C. Isaiah prophesied that Cyrus the Persian would allow the Jews to return from Babylon after the exile (44:28). His words were fulfilled 176 years later in 536 B.C. When Persia conquered Babylon, Cyrus issued a decree that the exiled Jews could return to Israel. (His decree is recorded in Ezra 1:1-4.) The Persian government actually paid for the restoration of Jerusalem and the rebuilding of the Temple as recorded in the Books of Ezra and Nehemiah.

In 553 B.C. Daniel described the future coming of Alexander the Great without mentioning him by name, the Grecian empire and his untimely death at a young age. Daniel's words were fulfilled 220 years later in 323 B.C. when Alexander died prematurely. His swift and fierce conquest, as described by Daniel, enabled him to conquer the known world at the time.

Isaiah describes the coming of John the Baptist 700 years in advance (40:1-5). John would come in the spirit and power of Elijah as the forerunner of the Messiah (Malachi 4:5, 6).

A Spiritual Book

The Bible is a spiritual book, not a scientific or philosophical book. It certainly contains science, history and philosophy as it tells the story of human history. But the Bible presents one essential truth, which is interwoven throughout every page—God loves us with an everlasting love and has provided salvation from our sins. The Bible addresses our deepest spiritual need—the need of forgiveness and reconciliation with God.

Standing the Test of Time

The Bible has stood the test of opposition on every front. The Bible thrives, in spite of *political pressure* down through the centuries. In A.D. 303 the Roman Emperor Diocletian burned every Bible he could confiscate and erected a column in his victory over Christianity bearing the inscription, "Extinct is the name of Christian." But in A.D. 312, Emperor Constantine became a Christian and elevated Christianity as the state religion in A.D. 325. He offered monetary rewards for any existing Bibles that could be found. Within two days, over 50 Bibles were brought out of hiding.

Joseph Stalin ordered that every copy of the Bible in Russia be confiscated. Today, Russia is flooded with Bibles, and a great revival of the Christian faith is storming Eastern Europe where the darkness of communism once reigned.

The Bible stands triumphant against *philosophical opposition.* Voltaire, the French philosopher, boasted, "Within a hundred years the Bible will be forgotten and eliminated." He died in 1778. Fifty years later, the Geneva Bible Society purchased Voltaire's home as its headquarters to print and distribute Bibles around the world.

Thomas Paine boasted that he had gone through the Bible revealing its lack of integrity. He claimed the Bible would cease to prosper. He died a drunkard in 1809. The Bible lives on.

The Bible has endured *religious persecution.* The Bible has been burned, banned and scorned. William Tyndale (1484-1536) printed the first English copy of the New Testament in 1525. The King James Version is basically a fifth revision of Tyndale's manuscript. His desire was to put the Bible in the hands of every person. Tyndale was executed for his work on Friday, October 6, 1535. The Bishop of London burned as many of the Tyndale's Bibles as possible.

Archaeology and History

Archaeology has always been the friend of the Bible. The famous Dead Sea Scrolls, discovered in a cave outside the Qumran community in the desert south of Jerusalem in 1947, confirm the accuracy of the Bible as we have it today. Most impressive is the scroll of Isaiah in its complete form which, when examined, is in complete harmony with the King James Version.

The ancient city of Dan was considered by many scholars to be fictitious until the 1970s, when a team led by Avraham Biran uncovered the *bamah*, a 60-square-foot sanctuary in Dan. Thousands of artifacts were also found. Most important was the discovery of the 45-foot arched gateway leading into the city. I have visited the city of Dan and have seen the splendor of this ancient site.[3]

In 1980 Israeli archaeologist Adam Zertal uncovered the altar of Joshua on Mount Ebal (see Joshua 8:30-35). The altar is constructed according to God's exact directives to Moses in Exodus 20:24-26. Moses commanded the Israelites to build an altar on Mount Ebal immediately after Joshua led them into the Promised Land (see Deuteronomy 27:2-8).

Along with the discovery was the exciting find of an Egyptian-style scarab. Within an oval frame, the scarab displays a geometrical pattern consisting of a four-petal rosette and between the petals, four branches. From each branch comes a uracus (an Egyptian cobra). The scarab is very rare and was dated between the period of Rameses II and Rameses III, or the last third of the 13th century B.C. This is the period that most believe marked the beginning of the Israelite settlement under Joshua. It was from the city of Rameses in the eastern Nile delta that the Israelites started their Exodus.

Remember the story of the Tower of Babel? Archaeologists have excavated over 24 temple towers, called *ziggurats*, in Mesopotamia just like the one Nimrod and his followers built as recorded in Genesis 11.

The Bible says that Abraham, the father of the Hebrew people, lived in a city called Ur of the Chaldees around 2000 B.C. Excavations conducted between 1922-1924 show that when Abraham left the city, it was at the height of commercial splendor and pagan idolatry.

In 1990, Harvard researchers working in Ashkelon uncovered a small silver-plated bronze calf figurine, reminiscent of the golden calf mentioned in Exodus.

In 1986 archaeologists found the earliest known text of the Bible, dated about 600 B.C. It suggests that parts of the Old Testament were written soon after some of the events described, as opposed to being written centuries later as some liberal scholars suggest.

In 1986 scholars identified an ancient seal that belonged to Baruch, the scribe, who recorded the prophecies of Jeremiah in 587 B.C.

In 1993 a team of archaeologists uncovered a ninth-century-B.C. inscription at an ancient mound called Tel Dan, in northern Israel, bearing the words "House of David," and "King of Israel." It was the first time David's name had been found outside the Bible, validating his existence. In 1995, the French scholar Andre Lemaire detected a phrase to the "House of David" on the Mesha Stele (also called the Moabite Stone) originally discovered in 1868 at the ruins of the Biblical site, Dibon. This is the second mention of David discovered outside the Bible.

In 1979, Israeli archaeologist Gabriel Barkay found two tiny silver scrolls inside a Jerusalem tomb. They were dated to around 600 B.C. shortly before the destruction of Solomon's temple and the Babylonian exile. When scientists carefully unrolled the scrolls at the Jerusalem Museum, they found a benediction from the Book of Numbers etched into their surface. The discovery made it clear that parts of the Old Testament were being copied long before some skeptics had believed they were written.

In 1990 Frank Yurco, an Egyptologist at the Field Museum of Natural History, used hieroglyphic clues from a monolith known as the Merneptah Stele to identify figures in a Luxor wall relief as ancient Israelites. The stele itself, dated to 1207 B.C., certifies that the Israelites were a distinct population more than 3,000 years ago.

Jeffery L. Sheler, in his article titled "Is the Bible True?" attests to the archaeological validity of Biblical history. He points out that not only has archaeology supported the Bible, the Bible has shed light on archaeology and history. Many archaeologists have made their discoveries by reading the Biblical record.[4]

Yigael Yadin, the Israeli archaeologist who excavated at Hazor in the 1950s, relied heavily on the Bible to find the great gate of Solomon at the famous upper Galilee site. "We went about discovering [the gate] with the Bible in one hand and a spade in the other," he said. Trude Dothan notes, "Without the Bible, we wouldn't even have known there *were* Philistines."⁵

The remains of Caiaphas were discovered in a burial cave near Jerusalem by archaeologists in November 1990. Twelve ossuaries, receptacles for the bones of the dead, dating back to the first century were found. Keys to identifying the remains of people include the elaborateness of the vault in which the bones were found and the inscription found in two places: "Joseph, son of Caiaphas." Caiaphas was the high priest who tried Jesus. He was in office between A.D. 18 and 36. Along with the remains, a bronze coin minted in the years A.D. 42 and 43 during the reign of Herod Agrippa I, was also found in another ossuary at the site.⁶

Science and the Bible

Science can be defined as the study of observable data. But can the Bible and science travel together?

The Bible refutes ancient cosmogony by revealing God as Creator.⁷ The ancient Chaldean theory of the origin of the universe viewed the earth as a gigantic monster, covered with feathers and scales (the rocks and the trees). The human race lives on the hide of this big monster as fleas live on a dog's back. If we burrow down too far, the monster will shake itself and everything we build will fall. They held this belief because they correlated their digs with earthquakes.

The Babylonian theory of creation claimed that in the beginning there was a monster named Tia-mat and a great god named Marduk. They had a fierce battle and Marduk conquered Tia-mat. When Marduk flattened out Tia-mat, his body became the earth. Then, Marduk spit and everywhere he spat, men came up. And then the men spat, and women came up. And then the women spat and animals came up.

The ancient Egyptians believed the world was held up by five great pillars, one at each corner of the earth and one in the middle. The Egyptian creation account states that the earth was hatched from a great cosmic egg, an egg with wings that was flying in space. As it flew, the processes of mitosis on the inside were completed and out hatched our world.

Moses records no such story. Although Moses was educated in the science of the Egyptians (Acts 7:22), he writes, "In the beginning God created the heavens and the earth" (Genesis 1:1).

The ancient Hindus believed the earth was flat and held up by three elephants, each standing on the other's back. What holds up the elephants? A giant turtle.

The Bible also records some interesting facts about the universe and our world. It records that the earth is spherical, not flat (Isaiah 40:22). The earth is suspended in space (Job 26:7). The stars are innumerable (Genesis 15:5; Hebrews 1:12). There are mountains and canyons in the sea (2 Samuel 22:16). The Bible accurately identifies the hydrological cycle (Job 26:8; Ecclesiastes 1:6, 7).

According to Genesis, every species reproduces after its own kind. Louis Pasteur (1862) and Gregor Johann Mendel (1865) empirically validated this truth in contrast to Aristotle's theory of spontaneous generation.

The Bible presents scientific facts centuries before man acknowledges them. God asks Job, "Can you bring forth the constellations in their seasons, or lead out the Bear with its cubs?" (38:32). Or "guide Arcturus with his sons?" as it reads in the King James Version. Arcturus is a runaway star system moving at 257 miles per second (our sun moves about 12 1/2 miles a second).

S.I. McMillen, M.D., in *None of These Diseases,* shows the accuracy of the medical, dietary and agricultural laws given in the Pentateuch. The Bible contains important medical laws such as sanitation laws (see Deuteronomy 23:12, 13), treatments for contagious disease (see Leviticus 14) and the importance of circumcision (see Genesis 17:9-14). Studies show that in relations between men and women, circumcision lowers cervical cancer in women, and the eighth day after a baby boy is born is the best day for the procedure because of the blood-clotting capacity.[8]

The Old Testament gives guidance for surgical cleanness. The priests were taught to wash their hands in running water and dry them in the sun to kill any remaining bacteria (see Leviticus 22:4-8). Modern medicine adopted this ancient procedure in the early 20th century, which led to the abolishment of infections often occurring from surgery. The Book of Leviticus accurately records that the human bloodstream is the source of life (17:11).

How Can We Know the Bible Is Accurate?

While skeptics question the accuracy of the Bible, the ancient texts have been copied from generation to generation with utmost care and integrity. No other religion has ever sought to maintain such integrity in its writings than have the Jews and the Christians. The early Christians were Jewish and came out of the tradition of preserving their sacred writings with utmost integrity.

An understanding of the Hebrew Talmudic rules for copying will dispel any uncertainty about the accuracy of the Bible. Stringent rules applied for copying the ancient texts. Each column contained no less than 48 and no more than 60 lines; no word or letter could be written from memory, but the scribe must have an authentic copy before him; one mistake condemned the sheet, and three mistakes on any page condemned the entire manuscript.

It is said that the older rabbi gave the solemn warning to each young scribe: "Take heed how you do your work, for your work is the work of heaven; lest you drop or add a letter of a manuscript and so become a destroyer of the world." Some texts were annotated, that is, each letter in each line was individually counted and totaled to make sure the texts were copied identically.

Let's turn our attention to the manuscripts. Fifteen hundred years after Herodotus wrote his history, there remained only one copy of his work in the entire world. Only half of one percent of all books published will survive seven years. Eighty percent of all books are forgotten within a year of publication.

I want to make a few comparisons between other significant historical writings and the Biblical manuscripts to make my point on the Bible's accuracy. Plato's writings (c. 375 B.C.) still intrigue those interested in philosophy. The latest manuscripts of his work date back to only A.D. 900, with only seven copies in existence.

The same is true for Aristotle (c. 330 B.C.). The oldest copies of his work are dated at A.D. 1100, with only five copies of manuscripts in existence. The earliest manuscript of the historical writings of Tacitus date back to

1,000 years after his death with only 20 copies in existence. Yet, we trust the historical writings of Tacitus. The earliest manuscript of Caesar's *Gaelic Wars* dates back to 1,000 years after the original was written.

Skeptics don't question the accuracy and validity of these writings. But there are some 5,000 Greek manuscripts and 8,000 Latin manuscripts of the New Testament, most of which are dated between A.D. 330-480. There are also fragments of New Testament books dated as early as 20 to 40 years after Christ's ascension. The Bible has more early manuscripts verifying its accuracy than any other book ever written.

The Book That Changed the World

Western civilization is founded on the principles of the Bible. The origin of Western civilization dates back to Paul's second missionary journey when he was directed by the Holy Spirit to travel to Europe to evangelize.

George Washington said, "It is impossible to rightly govern the world without God and the Bible." Abraham Lincoln said, "I believe the Bible is the best gift God has ever given to man. All the good from the Savior of the world is communicated to us through this Book."

Immanuel Kant said, "The existence of the Bible, as a book for people, is the greatest benefit which the human race has ever experienced. Every attempt to belittle it is a crime against humanity."

In a *Newsweek* article titled, "How the Bible Made America," the authors observe that the Bible has for centuries "exerted an unrivaled influence on American culture, politics and social life. Now historians are discovering that the Bible, perhaps even more than the Constitution, is our founding document: the source of the powerful myth of the United States as a special, sacred nation, a people called by God to establish a model society, a beacon to the world."[9]

They go on to say, "There were times, too, when Bible study was the core of public education and nearly every literate family not only owned a Bible, but read from it regularly and reverently." Because of this pervasive Biblical influence, the United States seemed to Europeans to be one vast congregation, as G.K. Chesterton said, "with the soul of a church."

James Russell Lowell, former minister of state for the United States to England, attended a banquet where Christianity was being attacked. He spoke up:

> I challenge any skeptic to find a 10-square-mile spot on this planet where they can live their lives in peace and safety and decency, where womanhood is honored, where infancy and old age are revered, where they can educate their children, where the gospel of Jesus Christ has not gone first to prepare the way. If they can find such a place, then I would encourage them to emigrate thither and there proclaim their unbelief. [10]

Our calendar and holidays are based on the Bible. So is our judicial system, which seeks to blend the principles of justice and mercy with utmost balance.

The Bible shaped the literary works of such authors as Shakespeare, Milton, Longfellow and Kipling. Michelangelo was moved by the Biblical themes to create such masterpieces as the painting on the ceiling of the Sistine Chapel

229

and sculptures of David, Moses and the Pieta. "The Last Supper," by da Vinci, and the works of such painters as Rembrandt, Raphael and many others continue to inspire the world.

The Bible has inspired musical masterpieces for centuries. Handel composed *The Messiah* using quotes from 15 Biblical books. Over 500,000 Christian hymns have been written since the birth of the church.

What other religious writings can compare with the stirring drama of creation recorded in Genesis . . . the moral code of the Ten Commandments . . . the comforting words of the Twenty-third Psalm . . . the ageless wisdom of the Beatitudes . . . the soul-stirring account of Christ's crucifixion and triumphant resurrection . . . the majestic prophetic preview of eternity as seen by John the Revelator?

Those who read it and take it to heart are changed forever by its power. "For the word of God is living and active. Sharper than any double-edged sword, it penetrates even to dividing soul and spirit, joints and marrow; it judges the thoughts and attitudes of the heart" (Hebrews 4:12).

When the Reformer Martin Luther was asked what role he thought he played in the Protestant Reformation, he replied, "I simply read, preached and taught the Word of God. Besides that, I did nothing. The Word did it all."

Captain Mitsuo Fuchida was the Japanese naval air commander who led the bombing attack on Pearl Harbor. He tells of the time after the war was over when the Japanese prisoners were returning home from America. He wondered what kind of treatment they had received.

One prisoner of war he questioned told how the prisoners were able to release their hate and hostility toward the Americans. He said that a young girl had shown kindness to the prisoners, who wondered why she was so good to them. They were shocked when she told them that it was because her parents were killed by the Japanese army. Her parents were missionaries in the Philippines when the war broke out, but when the Japanese invaded, they were forced to flee to the mountains.

Later, they were found, tried for being spies and executed. Before they were killed, they asked for 30 minutes to pray, which was granted. The girl was sure they had spent that time praying for the forgiveness of their executioners. Because of this, she allowed the Holy Spirit to remove the hatred from her heart and replace it with forgiveness.

As Fuchida listened to this POW's story, he could not understand such love. Several months passed, and one day in Tokyo he was handed a gospel tract as he left a train station. It told the story of Sergeant Jacob DeShazer, who was captured and tortured by the Japanese army, and held prisoner for 40 months. In prison camp, he received Christ by reading the Bible. God's Word removed the bitterness from his heart and enabled him to forgive his enemies. After the war was over, DeShazer returned to Japan as a missionary.

Fuchida was stirred by the power of this love he kept hearing about. So he bought a Bible and began reading it. He came to the Crucifixion scene and was struck by Jesus' prayer from the cross, "Father, forgive them; for they know not what they do." Jesus prayed for the very soldiers who had nailed him to the cross. Fuchida's heart broke under the compelling force of Christ's love, and became a follower of Jesus Christ. He later wrote his testimony in his book *From Pearl Harbor to Golgotha.*[11]

God promises, "My word . . . will not return to me empty, but will accomplish what I desire and achieve the purpose for which I sent it" (Isaiah 55:11).

11

Turning the World Upside Down

I t was the greatest crisis the disciples had ever faced. For three and a half years they had followed Jesus. They had forsaken all. They believed Him to be the Messiah, the Son of God. They had witnessed His exemplary life. No one ever lived as He lived or spoke as He spoke. They had witnessed His miracles—feeding the 5,000, healing the sick, driving out demons, raising the dead, walking on the water.

But all that was over now. The dream had ended. What could they do now but flee Jerusalem, return to their menial jobs and hope that they too wouldn't be arrested? For three days they locked themselves in an upper room, terrified that they would be found and face the same punishment Jesus had suffered. Suddenly, Jesus appeared in the room with them. "Peace be with you! As the Father has sent me, I am sending you" (John 20:21). They moved from confusion to a commission. They left that room empowered by the risen Christ to carry the gospel to the entire world.

233

Today, over 2 billion of the world's 6 billion population are devout followers of Jesus, and all other religions welcome Jesus. During the last five years of the 1990s, Christianity grew approximately 8 percent. An estimated 165,000 people come to know Christ every day. If this rate continues, nearly half the world's population will be Christian in only a few years.[1]

I took my first missions trip to Trinidad. I was a young pastor with a newly planted congregation, and wanted to embrace a global vision for our ministry. So I took a group of 10 people for two weeks of ministry in Trinidad. I will never forget the emotional impact that trip made on me. After finally getting through the airport, we traveled in small vans for about an hour to our destination. I fought back the tears as I saw and felt the deep spiritual need. I have never seen the world the same since.

Have you taken a good look at the world lately? Here is an e-mail I received:

> If the world were 100 people, there would be 57 Asians, 21 Europeans, 14 from North and South America, 8 Africans; 52 females, 48 males; 70 would be nonwhite, 30 white; 59 percent of the entire world's wealth would belong to only 6 people, and all 6 would be citizens of the U.S.; 80 would live in substandard housing, 70 would be unable to read, 50 would suffer from malnutrition, only 1 would have a college education, and 99 of them could not see this email message, because only 1 would have a computer.

In May 1792, a significant event transpired in Nottingham, England. William Carey stood before a group of ministers

and delivered what has been called the greatest missionary sermon in church history. In it he appealed for the
evangelization of all people. At that time there were no
missionary societies anywhere in the world. William
Carey made a map of the world, placed it on the wall of
his cobbler shop and began to pray for the whole world.

He became so burdened for the lost that he left home
and went to Bengal, India. He preached there for seven
years before he had his first Indian convert. Over the
years Carey translated the Bible, or parts of it, into 40 different Indian languages or dialects. Within a generation,
scores of young men and women had answered Christ's
call to carry the good news to the ends of the earth.

If evangelism is so important, what is it? To evangelize
simply means to tell the good news of Jesus Christ.
Evangelism is not the preaching of an idea, a system or a
principle, but a Person. Rather than being coerced, forced,
or manipulated, evangelism springs naturally from the
believer's heart that overflows with the love of God for
the world.

Evangelism is the outflow of the inner life. Jesus said,
"From [your] innermost being shall flow rivers of living
water" (John 7:38, *NASB*). And, "Out of the overflow of
the heart the mouth speaks" (Matthew 12:34). E. Stanley
Jones once said that the Holy Spirit is like electricity—
He never goes in where He can't come out!

A little boy came home from Sunday school a bit troubled, and said to his mother, "Mommy, my Sunday
school teacher told me today that if I invite Jesus into my
heart He would come in there and live in me."

His mother replied, "That's right, sweetheart, He will."

With a look of concern he said, "But, Mom, won't a lot of Him stick out?"

That's evangelism. A lot of Jesus sticks out!

Take an Adventure

Life with Christ is an adventure of ever-unfolding possibilities, challenges and opportunities. Jesus said, "Open your eyes and look at the fields! They are ripe for harvest" (John 4:35). Jesus promises us, "I have placed before you an open door that no one can shut" (Revelation 3:8).

How are we to respond to the opportunity? We can *isolate* ourselves from the world, as did the monastic order of the Middle Ages. We can *transcend* the world like the Pharisees of Christ's day. We can *ignore* the world by focusing inwardly on our own needs. We can *condemn* the world by pronouncing judgment. We can *forsake* the world, thinking that the problems of the day prevent the possibility of revival. Or, we can take action and *invade* the world with the love of God.

The first word of Christ's commission is *go*—"Go and make disciples of all nations" (Matthew 28:19). Immediately after Pentecost, the early church stayed in Jerusalem, although believers had been commissioned to go to the entire world. As far as they were concerned, the "world" meant their own private world, their own comfort zone.

There they stayed, enjoying the fellowship, the teaching and personal ministry. The people met together daily for worship and celebration (see Acts 2:42; 5:12). Prayers were answered. Healings occurred. Luke tells us what an incredible time it was: "All the believers were one in heart and mind. No one claimed that any of his possessions was his own, but they shared everything they had" (4:32). The church exploded with growth, "praising God and enjoying the favor of all the people. And the Lord added to their number daily those who were being saved' (2:47).

Something was missing, however. The longer they stayed, the more ingrown they became. Congregational contentions and administrative hassles began to surface. All along the Holy Spirit was nudging them to *go*.

Then a deacon by the name of Stephen was arrested for preaching Christ. When confronted by the high priest to answer charges of blasphemy, he delivered one of the most prophetic sermons recorded in the New Testament (see Acts 7). The punch line was anything but acceptable to his hearers: "You stiff-necked people, with uncircumcised hearts and ears! You are just like your fathers: You always resist the Holy Spirit!" (v. 51).

The incident resulted in the tragic stoning of Stephen. But in the midst of this tragedy, faith triumphed.

"Look," Stephen shouted, as stones were hurled at him, "I see heaven open and the Son of Man standing at the right hand of God" (v. 56).

As the last stone struck his body, he slumped to the ground and whispered his final prayer, "Lord, do not hold this sin against them" (v. 60).

What was meant for evil, God used for good. "On that day a great persecution broke out against the church at Jerusalem, and all except the apostles were scattered throughout Judea and Samaria" (8:1). Persecution became an instrument in the hand of the Holy Spirit to *scatter* the church. No longer would they be content to *stay*. From now on they would *go*.

As God scattered those early believers, He desires to scatter us. The apostle Peter calls believers "God's elect, strangers in the world, scattered" (1 Peter 1:1). The word *strangers* here means "those placed alongside of." God strategically places us in our families, workplaces, neighborhoods and communities as His witnesses.

The word *scattered* refers to scattering seed. God scatters His people throughout the world as a farmer scatters seed for harvest. Wherever you live, work and play is not coincidental. You have been scattered by God to be a living testimony of His love and grace.

Several years ago I read a challenging statement in an editorial in *Fortune* magazine: "What we of the world need is a word from the Lord. We look to the church for that word and all we hear is the echo of our own voices."

The gospel is the good news of the grace of God. The Christmas proclamation says it best: "Do not be afraid. I bring you good news of great joy that will be for all the people. . . . A Savior has been born to you; he is Christ the Lord" (Luke 2:10, 11).

> Go and share the good news . . .
> The Savior has come!
> Your sins are forgiven!
> Receive the free gift of eternal life!

One Sabbath, while worshiping at the Nazareth synagogue, Jesus stood before the people and read from the scroll of

Isaiah: "The Spirit of the Lord is on me, because he has anointed me to preach good news to the poor. He has sent me to proclaim freedom for the prisoners and recovery of sight for the blind, to release the oppressed, to proclaim the year of the Lord's favor" (Luke 4:18, 19).

Christ's message is our message. Go into your world with the confidence that the Spirit of the Lord is on you, because He has anointed you to preach good news!

We often feel inadequate, anxious, or even guilt-ridden when the subject of sharing our faith is mentioned. So, what skills do we need to help us turn our world upside down?

Compelling Love

When Jesus saw the crowds, "He had compassion on them, because they were harassed and helpless, like sheep without a shepherd" (Matthew 9:36).

In *The Art of Rhetoric*, Aristotle said the first mark of a persuasive communicator is emotion, or *pathos*, the root of the words *passion* and *compassion*. Paul said, "Christ's love compels us" (2 Corinthians 5:14).

In his writings, we sense Paul's deep passion for those who are lost spiritually: "I have great sorrow and unceasing anguish in my heart. For I could wish that I myself were cursed and cut off from Christ for the sake of my brothers. . . . My heart's desire and prayer to God for the Israelites is that they may be saved" (Romans 9:2, 3; 10:1).

Martin Luther said, "Every man is called to be Christ to his neighbor." In A.D. 252 a deadly plague broke out in the city of Carthage. Cyprian, the Christian bishop of the city, gathered his congregation together. They buried the dead and nursed the sick after the pagans had thrown out the bodies of their dead and fled the city for terror. The church saved the city at the risk of losing their lives. This is what the command, "Love your neighbor as yourself," means.

Earning the Right to be Heard

America is a nation of seekers. Gallup reports that 82 percent of Americans are on a spiritual search, and 51 percent say they have discussed spiritual matters in the previous 24 hours. This spiritual quest is taking place largely outside organized religion. The University of Chicago's National Opinion Research Center reports that in 1998, only 16 percent to 18 percent of 18- to 22-year-olds said they had any contact with organized religion in the previous year. Yet, 81 percent of them were asking spiritual questions such as, "What happens when I die?"[2]

Why is it that we usually think of sharing our faith in terms of talking to people of beliefs instead of listening to them about their beliefs? Proverbs 20:5, says, "The purposes of a man's heart are deep waters, but a man of understanding draws them out." It is our job to "draw them out" and learn why they hold their beliefs and convictions.

Tim Muehlhoff says, "Communication is a give-and-take proposition, a right to be earned." He suggests that we ask a seeker the following questions: *What experiences have led you to your current convictions? What individuals have influenced your thinking the most? When did you first start to think this way? How have your ideas changed over time?*[3]

Living the Faith

Faith begins with hearing, whether it is by mass media, literature, music, the arts, a church service, or personal testimony. Paul reminds us that "faith comes from hearing the message, and the message is heard through the word of Christ" (Romans 10:17).

The greatest impact of all is a life of integrity. Discipleship is caught as much as it is taught. William Barclay said, "The Christian dare not say, 'I care not what men say or think of me.' He must care—for his life is a testimony for or against his faith."

The British explorer Henry Morgan Stanley visited missionary David Livingstone in Africa. After having spent considerable time with him, he said, "If I had been with him any longer, I would have been compelled to be a Christian, and he never spoke to me about it at all."

Befriending Others

Our culture is interconnected electronically via the Internet, but disconnected emotionally and spiritually. Jesus was called the "friend of sinners" (Matthew 11:19). What was intended to be a criticism was actually a great compliment! Jesus went where the people were. He connected with them on a social level. He created the opportunity for evangelism.

One day He struck up a casual conversation with a dejected woman by Jacob's Well, which eventually led not only to her salvation but the salvation of many in her hometown (see John 4). You and I too have to become the friend of sinners.

Christians often make the mistake of insulating and isolating from the world. They spend all their time at church or Christian events, and lose touch with the world. We need to get out of the salt shaker and into the world!

How many unsaved friends do you have? How often do you interact with people who don't know Jesus? Your mission field is all around you. You don't have to go on a missions trip to do missions work, just open your eyes and look at the fields (see John 4:35).

The magnetism of Jesus was His unconditional love for everyone. People felt worthwhile, valuable, and important to God when Jesus was around. He met their deepest need—the need to love and to be loved. The love of God, which has been poured into our hearts, is the power to reach those who are lost.

Recently, a young woman walked into my office for a counseling appointment. As she began to share her story of pain and guilt, she paused and said to me, "The reason I came to see you is because I knew you would not judge me." The fruit of the Spirit is love. People are drawn to the healing power of Christ's love when we become friends of sinners.

Building a Bridge

People no longer accept information at face value. The breakdown of authority at all levels of society, as well as the influence of moral relativism, has bred a sense of skepticism. We want proof!

Open discussion is more effective than the hard sell approach. Believers need to know their faith so they can answer people's spiritual questions. Open discussion demonstrates respect for others' viewpoints and builds relationships. Dialogue opens the way for the Holy Spirit to do His work in human hearts.

Dialogue is easy to establish when we look for common ground. When I did my graduate work in psychology, I looked for common ground between personality theories and the Bible's view of human nature. The same needs to happen when sharing the faith with someone with different beliefs.

Tim Muehlhoff says, "The greatest skill needed by Christians entering the new millennium will not be the ability to debate, but the ability to recognize and affirm God's truth buried in the perspectives of our neighbors and friends. In the new millennium, differences will be apparent; it will take skill to cultivate common ground."[4] Look for areas where their perspectives, beliefs and values are compatible with Scripture to show that they may be closer to Christianity than they realize.

Try to close the gap between you and the person you are trying to reach. So many believers want to be prophets and confront the world. While there are true prophets, not every Christian is called to be one. But we are all called to be priests to minister the grace of Christ. The word *priest* means "a bridge-builder." Effective witnesses find ways to build bridges to reach others for Christ.

Extending Kindness

In his book *Conspiracy of Kindness,* Steve Sjogren tells the true story of Joe Delaney and his 8-year-old son Jared, who were playing catch in their backyard in the Cincinnati area. Jared asked, "Dad, is there a God?"

Joe told him that he had only gone to church a few times as a kid and wasn't really sure. Jared ran into the house. "I'll be right back!" he yelled. A few minutes later he returned with a helium balloon from the circus, a pen and an index card.

"I'm gonna send God an airmail message," Jared explained. "Dear God, if you are real and you are there, send people who know you to Dad and me."

God, I hope You're watching, Joe thought, as they watched the balloon and message sail away. Two days later, Joe and Jared pulled into a car wash sponsored by Sjogren's church.

Joe asked, "How much for a car wash?"

Steve said, "It's free."

"But why are you doing this?" Joe inquired.

"We just want to show God's love in a practical way," Sjogren answered.

"Are you guys Christians, the kind of Christians who believe in God?" Joe asked.

Sjogren said, "Yes, we're that kind of Christians."

From that meeting, Steve led Joe to accept Jesus Christ as Lord.

Persisting in Prayer

Remember to pray for the people with whom you share your faith. Paul E. Billheimer, in *Destined for the Throne,* says, "Prayer is not begging God to do something He loaths to do. It is not overcoming reluctance in God. It is enforcing Christ's victory over Satan. It is implementing upon earth heaven's decisions concerning the affairs of men. Calvary legally destroyed Satan, and canceled all of his claims."

He continues, "God placed the enforcement of Calvary's victory in the hand of the church (Matthew 18:18; Luke 10:17-19). He has given her 'power of attorney.' She is His 'deputy.' But this delegated authority is wholly inoperative apart from the prayers of a believing church. Therefore, prayer is where the action is."[5] The statement is true: "The fate of the world is in the hands of nameless saints." Nameless saints who pray faithfully.

George Mueller was a great man of faith who built and directed orphanages in England during the 1800s. He devoted his life to pray for five of his friends. After five years, one of his friends accepted Christ. After 10 years, two more were saved. After 25 years, a fourth was converted. He continued praying for his fifth friend until he himself died. The man received Christ a few months after Mueller's death. Mueller had prayed for that man for over 50 years.

"Let us not become weary in doing good, for at the proper time we will reap a harvest if we do not give up" (Galatians 6:9).

Taking the Final Step

Quite often we only get to plant the seed of the gospel when we share our faith. Someone else may have the opportunity of actually leading them to Christ. But always be ready to lead them to a point of decision. After you have determined where they are in their beliefs, ask the Holy Spirit to give you direction in how to lead them to a decision for Christ.

The gospel of Christ is a call for action. Jesus calls every person to believe and to follow Him. The important question to consider is, *What is the next step to bring this person closer to Jesus so that he or she will make a commitment to Him?*

Remember, above all, we are not sharing a set of religious beliefs; we are introducing our families, friends, neighbors and the world to Jesus Christ. The very mention of His name brings the power of heaven to move on a person's heart to receive Him by faith.

The largest crowd Charles Spurgeon ever addressed came the night he spoke in the Crystal Palace to a crowd of 23,654 people. A mutiny had occurred in India protesting Britain's rule over that land, and a service of national humiliation was planned. Spurgeon was selected to deliver the sermon.

The night before the service he went to the Crystal Palace to test the acoustics, since the building was not constructed with religious services in mind. As he stood on the platform he repeated the verse, "Behold the Lamb of God which takes away the sin of the world."

His words were heard by a man working somewhere in the building. The man came to Spurgeon several days later to say that those words had touched his heart. That night alone in the Crystal Palace he received Jesus Christ.[6]

Therefore, Go . . .

It is my prayer that the words of Jesus will resonate in your heart every day, *"Therefore, go . . ."* We cannot expect others to come to us searching for God; we must go to them. Every day we are being sent by Christ into the world to make disciples of everyone we meet.

Oliver Cromwell was Lord Protector of the Common-wealth of England, Scotland and Ireland during the civil war of the 17th century. During his administration, the treasury ran out of silver to mint coinage. Cromwell sent delegates throughout the empire to collect silver for the treasury to use. They reported back to Cromwell that the only silver they could find was in the statues of the saints in the churches and cathedrals.

"What should we do?" they requested.

Cromwell replied, "Melt the saints down and put them into circulation."

That's what Christ wants to do with every believer—melt us down, mold us into His image, and put us in circulation.

You and I can make a difference. Listen to Jesus' challenge in the Sermon on the Mount as recorded in *The Message:*[7]

> Let me tell you why you are here. You're here to be salt-seasoning that brings out the God-flavors of this earth. If you lose your saltiness, how will people taste godliness? You've lost your usefulness and will end up in the garbage.
>
> Here's another way to put it: You're here to be light, bring-ing out the God-colors in the world. God is not a secret to be kept. We're going public with this, as public as a city on a hill. . . . Shine! Keep open house; be generous with your lives. By opening up to others, you'll prompt people to open up with God, this generous Father in heaven (Matthew 5:13-16).

May our prayer be that of Jim Elliott, who gave his life carrying the gospel of Christ to the Auca Indians:

Lord, make me a crisis man.
Not just a signpost on the highway of life,
  but a fork in the road;
So that men who meet me will come to know Jesus
  Christ.

References

Introduction
[1]Quoted in *Christian Clippings* (August 1997) 17.

Chapter 1: The Invasion of Islam
[1]Bob Larson, *Larson's New Book of Cults* (Wheaton: Tyndale House, 1999) 92-94.

[2]Barbara C. Baker, "Taliban Threatens Converts," *Christianity Today* (March 5, 2001) 34.

[3]Bob Woodward, "FBI: Papers mix prayers, hijacker's to-do list," *Atlanta Journal-Constitution* (Friday, September 28, 2001) A20.

[4]Larson 92-96.

Chapter 2: Jesus And Judaism
[1]Adapted from Walter Elwell, ed., *Evangelical Dictionary of Theology* (Grand Rapids: Baker, 1984) 589, 590.

[2]See Luke 23:50-52; John 7:50-52; 19:38-42.

[3]See Jeremiah 23:5, 6; 30:8, 9; 33:14-17, 20, 21; Ezekiel 37:24, 25; Daniel 7:13, 14; Hosea 3:4, 5; Amos 9:11; Zechariah 14:4, 9.

[4]See Matthew 26:26-30; Hebrews 8:7-13.

[5]See Hebrews 4:14-16; 9:11-15; 10:11-18.

[6]William Barclay, *Jesus As They Saw Him* (Grand Rapids: Eerdmans, 1962) 111-152.

Chapter 3: Is the East Really Enlightened?
[1]Larson 61-64.

[2]Paul L. Walker, *Is Christianity the Only Way?* (Cleveland, TN: Pathway, 1975) 67-70.

[3]Larson 70-78.

Chapter 4: What's New About New Age?

[1]Robert Lindsey, "Spiritual Concepts Drawing a Different Breed of Adherent," *New York Times* (September 29, 1986) R13.

[2]Fergus M. Bordewich, "Colorado's Thriving Cults," *The New York Times Magazine* (May, 1988) 37-46.

[3]Bordewich 37-46.

[4]Daniel L. Black, "The Familiar and Deceptive Language of the New Agers," *Evangel Magazine* (October, 1992) 7.

[5]Adapted from Larson 365-367.

[6]Sharon Beekman, "Deliver Us From Evil." *Moody* Magazine. (March/April, 1996). Reprinted with permission.

Chapter 5: Stars, Cards and Psychics

[1]Jeffrey L. Sheler, "The Christmas Covenant," *U.S. News & World Report* (December 19, 1994) 64.

[2]Adapted from D. James Kennedy, *The Real Meaning of the Zodiac* (Ft. Lauderdale: TCRM, 1993) 6.

[3]Larson 141.

[4]Kennedy 143, 144.

[5]William Barclay, *The Revelation of John, Volume 2* (Philadelphia: Westminster, 1976) 214, 215.

[6]Kennedy 14, 15; 153, 154.

[7]R.M. Enroth, "The Occult," *Evangelical Dictionary of Theology*, Walter A. Elwell, ed. (Grand Rapids: Baker House, 1984) 787, 788.

[8]Enroth 787.

[9]Enroth 788.

[10]Russell Chandler, *Understanding the New Age* (Dallas: Word Publishing, 1988) 356, 359.

Chapter 6: When the Mormons Come Knocking

[1]Jeffery L. Sheler, "The Mormon Moment," *U. S. News & World Report* (November 13, 2000) 59-65.

[2]Sheler, "The Mormon Moment" 59-65.

[3]Sheler, "The Mormon Moment" 59-65.

[4]Walter Martin, *The Kingdom of the Cults* (Minneapolis: Bethany

House, 1985) 190, 191

    [5]Martin 191.

    [6]Larson 308-317.

    [7]Larson 308-317.

    [8]Larson 311.

    [9]Sheler, "The Mormon Moment" 62.

    [10]Sheler, "The Mormon Moment" 57.

    [11]Francis J. Beckwith, "With a Grain of Salt, *Christianity Today* (November 17, 1997) 57, 58.

    [12]Larson 313.

    [13]Sheler, "The Mormon Moment" 65.

    [14]Larson 313.

    [15]Bechwith 57.

    [16]Larson 313, 314.

    [17]Gaebelein 535.

    [18]Beckwith 58.

    [19]Sheler, "The Mormon Moment" 62

    [20]Keith L. Brooks, *The Spirit of Truth and the Spirit of Error* (Chicago: Moody, 1976) 213.

    [21]Martin 205.

    [22]Martin 219.

    [23]Sheler, "The Mormon Moment" 65.

    [24]Larson 314.

    [25]See Hebrews 4:14-16; 7:1-25; 8:1-6.

    [26]Sheler, "The Mormon Moment" 62.

    [27]Sheler, "The Mormon Moment" 63.

    [28]Quoted in Karl Alsin, "When the Cults Come Knocking" *Discipleship Journal* (Issue 115, 2000) 28-32.

Chapter 7: Who Are the Jehovah's Witnesses?

    [1]*Watchtower,* September 15, 1910

    [2]Larson 269.

    [3]Martin 50.

    [4]Martin 72, 73.

    [5]Larson 269.

    [6]Martin 72.

[7]Anthony A. Hoekema, *The Four Major Cults* (Grand Rapids: Eerdmans, 1963) 238, 239.

[8]Martin 75.

[9]*Watchtower,* September 15, 1910.

[10]Edmund C. Gruss, *Jehovah's Witnesses—Their Monuments to False Prophecy* (Clayton, CA: Witness, 1997) 176.

[11]Martin 50.

[12]Martin 99.

[13]Martin 120.

[14]*The Truth Shall Make You Free* (The Watch Tower Bible and Tract Society, 1943), 295.

[15]Larson 270-272.

[16]*Watchtower*, May 1, 1976.

[17]Larson 272.

[18]Keith L.Brooks, *The Spirit of Truth and the Spirit of Error* (Chicago: Moody, 1976) 163.

[19]Martin 121.

[20]Larson 271.

[21]Larson 270, 271.

[22]Mark A. Kellner, "Watch Tower Undergoes Corporate Shakeup," *Christianity Today* (March 5, 2001) 35.

[23]Kelner 35.

[24]William J. Schnell, *Thirty Years a Watch Tower Slave* (Grand Rapids: Baker, 1956) 59.

[25]Schnell 19.

Chapter 8: In Search of Jesus

[1]George Gallup, Jr. and Timothy Jones, *The Next American Spirituality* (Colorado Springs: Victor, 2000) 14-19.

[2]Michael Green, *Who Is This Jesus?* (Nashville: Oliver-Nelson Books, 1990) 113-118.

[3]Dian Fossey, *Gorillas in the Mist*, (New York: Mariner Books, 2000) 34.

[4]Green 118.

Chapter 10: Can We Trust the Bible?

[1]Robert J. Hutchinson, "The Jesus Seminar Unmasked," *Christianity Today* (April 29, 1996) 28-30.

[2]Henry C. Thiessen, *Lectures in Theology* (Grand Rapids: Eerdmans Publishing, 1979) 63-66.

[3]Marlin Levin, "The Fabled City of Dan," *Discover* (November, 1980) 56-59.

[4]Jeffery L. Sheler, "Is The Bible True?" *U.S. News & World Report* (October 25, 1999) 50-59.

[5]Sheler 50-59.

[6]Ronny Reich, "Caiaphas' Name Inscribed on Bond Boxes," *Biblical Archaeology Review* (September/October, 1991) 38-44.

[7]Adapted from a sermon by W.A. Criswell entitled, "The Infallible Word of God," published in *Passion for Preaching,* complied by David L. Olson (Nashville: Thomas Nelson, 1989) 37-46.

[8]S. I. McMillen, *None of These Diseases* (Old Tappan: Spire Books, 1986).

[9]Kenneth L. Woodward with David Gatest and bureau reports, "How the Bible Made America," *Newsweek* (December 27, 1982) 44-51.

[10]James Fredinand S. Schenck, *Christian Evidences and Ethics* (New York: Young Men's Christian Association Press, 1910) 85.

[11]Billy Graham, *How To Be Born Again* (Waco: Word, 1977) 125-126.

Chapter 11: Turning the World Upside Down

[1]*Net Results* (August 2000) 20.

[2]Dick Staub, "How to Influence Your World," *Discipleship Journal* (Issue 122, 2001) 41- 49.

[3]Tim Muehlhoff, "Can Your Relate?" *Discipleship Journal* (Issue 122, 2001) 61-65.

[4]Muehlhoff 62.

[5]Paul E. Billheimer, *Destined For The Throne* (Fort Washington: Bethany House, 1975) 18.

[6]Arnold Dallimore, *Spurgeon* (Chicago: Moody Press, 1984) 94.

[7]Eugene H. Peterson, *The Message: The New Testament, Psalms and Proverbs* (Colorado Springs: NavPress, 1995).